# THIS
# GOSPEL
# REVOLUTION

*Unveiling Jesus and the
coming glory*

## SAM ORE

**THIS GOSPEL REVOLUTION:**
**Unveiling Jesus and the coming glory**

ISBN: 978-1-7327483-0-9

Copyright © 2018

**Collustrations Media LLC**
In collaboration with
**Sam Ore Ministries**
1813 Long Leaf Way
Servern MD 21144
www.collustrations.com
Email: project@collustrations.com

**Edited by:**
Kayode Olawuyi

# CONTENTS

**DEDICATION**                                         6

**INTRODUCTION**                                       7
My Epiphany

**CHAPTER ONE**                                       13
The Trinitarian Vision: Full Cycle

**CHAPTER TWO**                                       21
What is your Spiritual Diet?: Theology

**CHAPTER THREE**                                     27
The god of the fallen Adam or the Father of the Risen
Jesus: Uncertainty

**CHAPTER FOUR**                                      36
The Only Gospel: Jesus Plus Nothing

**CHAPTER FIVE**                                      43
Jesus in the Entire Cosmos: The Ubiquitous Nature of Jesus:

**CHAPTER SIX**     **59**
Jesus in the Entire Bible: Christology

**CHAPTER SEVEN**     **69**
These are not the Days of the Prophets: No Mixture

**CHAPTER EIGHT**     **83**
 Losing Members to the Church of Jesus Christ: True
Greatness

**CHAPTER NINE**     **97**
The Grace-made Generation: Babylon is Crumbling

**CHAPTER TEN**     **107**
The Collapse of the Religious Empire: The Coming
Splinter

**CHAPTER ELEVEN**     **113**
A Disruptive Awakening of the Spirit: Organized Chaos

**CHAPTER TWELVE**     **125**
On the Threshold of a Revolutionary Awakening: Tail Piece

**REFERENCE**     **136**

**CONTACT INFORMATION**     **137**

# DEDICATION

**T**his book is dedicated to God, my Heavenly Father. Thanks for revealing Jesus to me through the Holy Spirit. I am eternally grateful to you, Sir.

Debby, my dear wife and best friend for life, I thank you for being graceful. Your kind disposition makes the message real in my life. I love you for life my babe.

Dunamis, Faith, Nicole and Casey, our ever Godly children. I am so grateful to you guys for giving me the opportunity to practice on you how my Heavenly Father relates with me. I love you all more than words can articulate.

# INTRODUCTION:
## My Epiphany

I was raised by my loving parents, David and Emily Ore in a very strict, religious environment. I didn't get to know my father very well because he died when I was barely five. My mother, who was a choleric disciplinarian but a Jesus-loving woman, became the father and the mother at the same time for me and my siblings. We lived an average, decent life with my mom, the only covering we all had at the time until she was snatched away by the cold hand of death. I was about twelve years old. All my hope was gone.

I became angry, frustrated and disappointed at God. I couldn't understand why a loving God would take my parents away at such a tender age. The minister at the funeral compounded my problems when he said God does whatever He wants to do and you cannot question Him. I believe a major part of my emotional life died that day. I knew I had challenges with the tough way my mom was raising me because I was the rebellious black sheep of the family but the last thing I wanted God to do for her was to kill her.

My *enfant terrible* older brother, who later became a Christian, had to take the responsibility of looking after me until I could no longer cope with his "boring life" of born-again experience anymore and I left the house for the street with my gang members.

Fast-forward, after series of near death experiences in the wild life on the street, I received Jesus into my life as my Savior. But the glorious experience was short-lived because my local church in an attempt to "disciple" me unintentionally gave me a set of hard rules to keep in order to please God and make heaven. I tried my best but my best was never enough. I went back to the street and for another four years lived a more reckless lifestyle that cannot be described. By the special grace of God, I walked back into the loving arm of Jesus Christ on April 18, 1986. This time around, I had been introduced to the word of faith ministry which grounded me in my personal walk with God.

Being a stubborn and strong-willed person, I logically thought within myself that I will do whatever it requires to live holy for God even if it will mean paying penance for all the sins I had ever committed. I prayed for hours and embarked on several days of fasting. I was always in every service at my local church. I gave the little money I had. I volunteered as a church worker in almost all the ministries within the church until I became a pastor of one of the largest churches in the city. But I always hit a brick wall. I got to the end of the road, with mid-life crisis after endless rat races that culminated into a series of manifestations of lusts in my soul. I abused my loving wife verbally and emotionally. Talk about transfer of aggression. I crumbled inside and was flat. At this point, I couldn't take it anymore. I yelled out at God in frustrations, "I am tired of this…". I didn't care anymore. That was about seven years ago.

Contrary to what I had always believed that God will strike me dead for getting upset at Him, I heard a calm response that seemed to be saying, "Now that you are tired of trying, let me help you." For the first time after over two decades of ministry, Matthew 11:28-30 started making sense to me. *"Come to Me, all you who labor and are heavy laden, and I will give you rest. Take My yoke upon you and learn from Me, for I am [a]gentle and lowly in heart, and you will find rest for your souls. For My yoke is easy and My burden is light"*

The message translation is particularly more interesting.

*"Are you tired? Worn out? Burned out on religion? Come to me. Get away with me and you'll recover your life. I'll show you how to take a real rest. Walk with me and work with me—watch how I do it. Learn the unforced rhythms of grace. I won't lay anything heavy or ill-fitting on you. Keep company with me and you'll learn to live freely and lightly."* (Matthew 11:28-30, The Message Translation).

This was the beginning of a series of encounters with the

Holy Spirit that led to many questions I had always wanted to ask my heavenly Father. Questions like: can any human really attain the level of impeccable holiness in our flesh on this side of eternity? If yes, how long will it take us and how are we going to know when we get there? But religion has taught us that we can't ask questions especially from a higher authority. Never mind that Peter and the other disciples asked Jesus many questions. Never mind that our children even ask "stupid" questions and because we love them, we answer their questions. But God doesn't have time for stupid questions. Really? God have mercy!

By the special grace of God, I can boldly say that my quest to know more about this loving God led me to start questioning certain things I have always believed. I started seeing Jesus not just as Savior or Lord but as a friend, lover and my everything. Dear reader, the answers we are looking for in life are found in Jesus Christ through the help of the Holy Spirit whose main ministry among others is to glorify Jesus (John 16:14). From that time till now, each time I study my Bible, He shows me Jesus and His finished work of grace even using Old Testament scriptures.

This was the beginning of the revelation of God's grace to me personally. It was my epiphany. Of course, it has not been a bed of roses. Like Paul, the first apostle of grace, I was lonely for a few years in the backside of the wilderness of life from where the Father began to retrain me through His Spirit. It was very scary. It looks like almost everything I thought I knew about God was crumbling before me. You see, until we admit that a large chunk of our fundamental theological framework is faulty, we will inadvertently continue to reproduce a hopeless generation that may eventually discard Christianity because of frustration.

As I delved into a deeper study of Christology, I discovered that my heart and my head wrestled with a lot of life-changing practical truths even unto this day. But the reality of my experience is so profound that it cannot be denied. I cannot deny that this Christo-centric revelation is making me a better husband to my dear wife, a better father to my loving children, a better pastor to our congregation and a more loyal person to my friends around the world.

Truth be told, once in a while, I still have a relapse into legalism and old way of thinking which affects my behavior and makes me react to things in the flesh. But overall, this message is changing me from the inside out and I cannot deny it. I can boldly say that by the grace of God, I am now getting the grasp of what Paul was saying to the church in Galatia,

> *"I am crucified with Christ: nevertheless I live; yet not I, but Christ liveth in me: and the life which I now live in the flesh I live by the faith of the Son of God, who loved me, and gave Himself for me"* (Galatians 2:20, KJV).

A paraphrase of this scripture will read something like this "I am not the one living my life anymore, but Christ is the one living His life through me because He is in me and I am in Him…" In other words, if you see anything that is attractive in me, don't give me credit for it because I am not the one responsible but Christ in me. It is my prayer that the body of Christ and the whole world will have a revolutionary encounter with the true Jesus Christ by whom all and everything was created and through whom the whole cosmos revolves.

**Sam Ore**

Silver Spring, Maryland.

# *Chapter One*

> *The truth of the gospel is: Jesus Christ is not plan B. He is not even plan A. He is The Plan. The Only Plan. Without Him, there is no plan at all. He is not an auxillary. There is no world without Him.*

## The Trinitarian Vision:
## FULL CYCLE

## CHAPTER
# ONE

## The Trinitarian Vision:
# FULL CYCLE

The Trinity is not a concept, it is an eternal reality of a mutually exclusive union of love, harmony, peace and grace. The Father, the Son and the Spirit co-existed in a timeless eternity. They live in eternity and eternity lives in them at the same time. This union of perfect love has an origin of harmonious musical experience of a peaceful, circular dance known as *perichoresis* in the original Hebrew language. This great dance is devoid of fear, anxiety or rancor because perfect love casts out fear (1 John 4:18).

Because perfect love is generous and not selfish, they decided to invite members of the human race into this circle which was the motivation for the word *"...And God said let us create man in our image..."* (Genesis 1:26). It is imperative to know that "God" in this verse is the word

ELOHIM in the Hebrew which is the word that describes the plural side of God. The pronouns "us" and "our" suggest that the Father was not just talking to Himself alone. The Father, the Son and the Spirit took the decision to include man in their union in an unbreakable consensus.

It is imperative that the man that will be invited into this union must have certain characteristics like the Father, the Son and the Spirit in order to be able to relate intelligently. Therefore, he must be created in their image and likeness. He must also be given an irrevocable ability to make choices which must be respected even when those choices are wrong. But because the core nature of this celestial family is love, they can't stop loving the man.

It should also not be forgotten that the Trinity is omniscient with a nature to know and foresee all things. They knew even before man was created that he was going to be seduced out of the party by a fallen angel called Lucifer. One of them, Jesus Christ decided to be the lamb that was slain even before there was anything called sin. That was in eternity past before there was Adam and Eve. Before there was anything called a tree. Before there was a fruit. Before there was disobedience. Before there was a fall. The mystery of redemption actually started before anything was lost.

The modern church has always presented the gospel as if Jesus was an afterthought or a plan B, as if the fall messed up God's original plan and the Trinity panicked and they hurriedly hacked an emergency plan B to rescue man after the fall.

The truth of the gospel is, Jesus Christ is not plan B. He is not even plan A. He is The Plan. The Only Plan. Without Him, there is no plan at all. He is not an auxillary. There is no world without Him. As we shall see in the following chapters, without Him, the entire cosmos disintegrates.

In our warped theology, we have been made to believe that Adam and Eve were punished by God and sent out of the garden. Because most of what we have been taught about God have been seen from a punitive sense of justice of an angry God.

The truth is that everything God did for Adam and Eve before and after they fell, was an act of grace. He provided them with everything they would need including dominion on the earth without them asking. After the fall, He soaked them in the blood of an innocent animal figuratively symbolizing the ultimate sacrifice of Jesus on Calvary cross. He sent them away from the garden so that they would not eat from the tree of life and live in their sinful and fallen state and be eternally banished from the Trinitarian circle. How are all these punishments? You see, the lens with which we read the Bible is very crucial. Are we being taught about the god of Adam after the fall or the Father that Jesus came to reveal? Adam's theology of God has been skewed after eating the fruit. His view of God has been discolored. The friendly Father, loving and compassionate God has been turned into a furious, judgmental and wicked god trying to kill them which was why they were hiding. Adam and Eve had changed but not God. For He is eternally consistent and unchangeable.

This message of God's amazing grace is as old as time itself. For indeed, grace was before creation. Grace existed before there was a molecule, atom, galaxy or milky way. The grace of God is as old as the Father, the Son and the Spirit. Therefore, grace is not a new vogue. Neither is it a movement, fad nor new revelation. God started the story of mankind with grace and He is going to wind up the age with grace. Grace, like other things God does, is going full cycle because God is the Alpha and the Omega and also everything in between. He sees the end from the beginning. He always seems to start from where He ends. We are born as infants looking for love and acceptance. We go from infancy into adolescence. From being single to being married with children. Children grow up and leave the house to start their own families and we become empty nesters. A day comes at old age when one of the couple dies and the other one becomes lonely again and later disappears.

There is the full cycle of times and seasons. From fall to winter. From winter to spring, from spring to summer and from summer to fall again. We have morning, afternoon and night and then morning again. The full cycle of giving and receiving is clearly stated in the Bible.

*"While the earth remains, Seedtime and harvest, Cold and heat, Winter and summer, And day and night Shall not cease"* (Genesis 8:22).

The point is, our heavenly Father in the scheme of things began unfolding His plans for humanity through grace and He is ending with grace on a much better and more glorious note because the glory of the latter house shall always be greater than the former.

The first Adam started by grace but ended in self occupation while the last Adam (Jesus) deleted Adam's race and finished His work by grace.

It has pleased the Father to execute His entire vision for us through Jesus by the anointing of the Holy Spirit. Jesus is at the center of their plan.

> *"For in him all things were created: things in heaven and on earth, visible and invisible, whether thrones or powers or rulers or authorities; all things have been created through him and for him".* (Colossians 1:16)

Even as powerful as the Holy Spirit is, He enjoys working in the background while putting the spotlight on the Son. He enjoys glorifying Jesus. And Jesus will say *"...The Spirit of the Lord is upon me..."* while the Father will say *"...This is my beloved son in whom I am well pleased, hear Him..."* (Matthew 17:5). And the Son will respond *"...whatever I hear my Father say is what I say..."* You see the alignment in the Trinitarian circle?

> Therefore, the entire Bible is about Jesus revealing the Father to us through the Spirit. Reading the Bible without seeing Him is a futile intellectual exercise with no life.

Therefore, the entire Bible is about Jesus revealing the Father to us through the Spirit. Reading the Bible without seeing Him is a futile intellectual exercise with no life.

*"But you do not have His word abiding in you, because whom He sent, Him you do not believe. You search the Scriptures, for in them you think you have eternal life; and these are they which testify of Me"* (John 5:38-39).

This book is all about Jesus and His finished work of Grace alone. Let's take the journey together as the Holy Spirit unveils Him to us as He reveals the heart of our Heavenly Father.

# Chapter Two

> *Our religious beliefs have been systematically developed over the years based on what we hear, feel, and perceive either through other people, our environment, authority figures or ancient traditions.*

## What Is Your Spiritual Diet?:
## THEOLOGY

CHAPTER
**TWO**

# What Is Your Spiritual Diet?:
# **THEOLOGY**

L et me make this clear at this point that I am not a professional theologian even though I have studied and researched different and brilliant theologians who have been a tremendous blessing to me on the subject of grace and Christo-centric gospel. This disclaimer is important because the purpose of this book is not to vilify anyone or organization. It is my own sincere attempt to add my voice in a pragmatic way to the ongoing revolution of the Jesus-centered message of grace that is sweeping through the earth.

Therefore, I will endeavor to avoid or simplify certain technical and theological dictions and verbiages that may be too complex for an average person who may just simply want to live a life that honors God. After all, I am writing for the masses of people that Jesus the Savior came to rescue.

A simple definition of theology is religious beliefs and theory when systematically developed. It is also the study of the nature of God and religious belief.

The two definitions above sum up the essential components of theology. The key phrases in the first definition are *religious beliefs* and *systematically developed*. While the key phrase in the second definition is *the study of the nature of God*. These primary words are very crucial within the context of theology.

Our religious beliefs have been systematically developed over the years based on what we hear, feel, and perceive either through other people, our environment, authority figures or ancient traditions. These belief systems form the basis of what we perceive to be God's nature. Any attempt by anyone to change this is usually resisted with everything we have even sometimes at the risk of our lives. Some view God as a God with a judicial retributive system who is seeking to inflict punishment or vengeance on someone for a wrong doing. Some other people may view God as the ultimate Creator of everything who has abandoned us to figure how to make the world a better place.

Whereas, some perceive God as a loving and gracious God who doesn't care the way they live even if it is reckless after all, He is a God of grace. There are some people who actually see God as an inconsistent authoritarian who can do anything He pleases with human beings anytime He chooses.

A recent Gallup organization polls show four different

ways average Americans view God. 31% believes God is authoritative: He is engaged in the world and He's judgmental. 16% thinks God is critical. He is judgmental and disengaged. 24% believes He is distant. He is not judgmental, but He is disengaged from our lives. The last group comprising of 24% believes God is benevolent. He is engaged in our daily lives and yet not judgmental. Essentially, 95% of people living in the Western culture have a murky view of God.

When Jesus asked the disciples in Matthew chapter 16 who they thought He was, He did not give them a multiple-choice test, He wanted a specific revelation of true theology. Peter got the right theology by revelation. This then confirms what Jesus said, *"All things have been delivered to Me by My Father, and no one knows the Son except the Father. Nor does anyone know the Father except the Son, and the one to whom the Son wills to reveal Him"* (Luke 10:22).

> The main job of every preacher, teacher or Bible scholar is to keep putting Jesus out there and leave the rest for the Holy Spirit to reveal. Therefore, every preacher to a certain degree must have the right theology. And who can give us the right theology except Jesus Himself.

The main job of every preacher, teacher or Bible scholar is to keep putting Jesus out there and leave the rest for the Holy Spirit to reveal. Therefore, every preacher to a certain degree must have the right theology. And who can give us the right theology except Jesus Himself. When people sit down to listen to sermons, they already believe something at the back of their minds. In most cases they are just looking for somebody to endorse what they already believe. One of the main jobs of a preacher therefore is to attack a false theology of God. Jesus did this effectively even to the point of death. But the challenge facing many preachers today is: how can you preach or teach what you don't understand yourself. There has to be a complete overhaul of our entire fundamental doctrine in order to embrace a theological deconstruct so we can start renewing our minds (Romans 12:1-2).

# Chapter Three

*Whether we will like to admit it or not. When Adam and Eve fell from grace in the garden, anxiety became the new default mindset of the human race.*

## The god of the fallen Adam or the Father of the risen Jesus?: UNCERTAINTY

CHAPTER
**THREE**

## The god of the fallen Adam or the Father of the risen Jesus?:
# UNCERTAINTY

It is very imperative that we understand that everyone has a theology with which they see God and relate with Him. The truth is that there is a default mindset that subconsciously interferes with the way we view God. Whether we will like to admit it or not. When Adam and Eve fell from grace in the garden, anxiety became the new default mindset of the human race. And anxiety produces fear which in turn creates either fight, flight or freeze. Little wonder why Adam and Eve were hiding behind the bushes (flight) and Adam blaming God for the woman He graciously gave him to help him (fight).

From that day forward, Adam and his race began to see God with another lens. Their theology became twisted and skewed. God was no longer the loving and friendly Father who will come in the evening to fellowship with them. He

■ 28 |

was now a terrifying, distant, hell-bent and vendetta-seeking God coming to get them to atone for their sins. Unfortunately, Adam and Eve's offspring and the entire human race inherited that warped mentality and legalistic mental ecosystem.

> *"This is the book of the genealogy of Adam. In the day that God created man, He made him in the likeness of God. He created them male and female, and blessed them and called them Mankind in the day they were created. And Adam lived one hundred and thirty years, and begot a son in his own likeness, after his image, and named him Seth."* (Genesis 5:1-3).

Because they had eaten from the tree of the knowledge of good and evil, the relationship of human beings with God would no longer be supernatural but mechanical based on the law of morality. Do good, get good. Do bad, get bad. But the trinity would not give up. They doubled down on their eternal vision that man will be rescued back into the Trinitarian circle. And because the incarnation is an irrevocable eternal reality for them, Jesus would emerge through a series of events, narratives, patriarchs, priests, prophets and kings, some of who spoke and prophesied in part about the Messiah. The amazing good news for the human race actually began after the fall when the Father declared in an intrepid verdict to satan, "the seed of the woman will bruise your head" (Genesis 3:15). The devil freaked out and in his confusion, tried his best to wage war against anything and everything that looks like that Seed.

It is therefore highly significant that the only thing to look for in the Bible is how everything comes together to reveal the Trinitarian's irrepressible vision and love in the Bible embodied in Jesus Christ. Reading and studying any other thing in the Bible without a revelation of Jesus in the unfolding of the original vision is a waste of time or at best an academic rigmarole which actually can be achieved in other books apart from the Bible. Interestingly, every other thing we are looking for is encapsulated in Jesus. Is it leadership? He is the greatest leader of all time. Is it wisdom? He is the wisdom of God. Is it true prosperity? He is everything. Talk about power. He created everything. See, any attempt to chase or pursue anything other than the person of Jesus and His finished work of grace alone will be tantamount to a promotion of religious thinking.

A good theology therefore is neither the optical illusion with which Adam and Eve plunged humanity into nor the bi-polar theory of the old testament saints who sometimes paint God as a schizophrenic deity who is loving today but may destroy you tomorrow. This is not because they meant harm but because they didn't have the all-knowing Holy Spirit in an ever-abiding manner in their ministries. They only had the anointing upon them but the believers in the new covenant have both anointing upon them and within them (1John 2:27). And that makes all the difference.

A perfect altruistic theology, is therefore the only one that Jesus the Son of God came to pontificate. He was so emphatic and so ironclad in His revelation of His Father's love and unrepentant understanding of Him that He drew a circle in the sand and dared the religious leaders and

Pharisees of the day to enter it if they knew anybody who knew the Father better than Him. *"No one knows the Father but the Son..."* (Luke 10:22). For the accuracy and the precision of our theology to be faultless, it is in our best interest to see God from the point of view or lens of Jesus. The old covenant saints as powerful, influential and revolutionary as they can be can never know God, the Father better than Jesus, the Son. No prophet or patriarch could possibly know the Father than the One who has always been with Him in the eternity past, present and future, who only manifested at the appointed time as God's incarnate.

> For the accuracy and the precision of our theology to be faultless, it is in our best interest to see God from the point of view or lens of Jesus.

Jesus Christ should never be an underdog in the world that was created by Him and for Him. He should never get so eclipsed under the shadows like a mere cosmic light weight and helpless gentle lamb. He is the gospel. We stand the risk of reducing the Bible to a book of dos and don'ts or a catalogue of information to achieve our purpose and dreams in life without an intimate relationship with Jesus. These legitimate desires to succeed in life are inherently activated as we engage the life transforming principles in God's word but to make those things the gospel without focusing on God's eternal love and grace is like missing the forest for the trees. The sad reality of this type of mindset is a lethargic lifestyle that makes God's children plod through life like spiritual orphans. Perhaps the saddest part of any Bible study, preaching or teaching without a focus on Jesus and His finished work of grace is a pseudo peace that is associated with such exercise.

It is even more laughable when a Christian's life and happiness is also directly connected to what the pagans seek after. We have so drifted away into the worldly system that everyday normal benefits from God to every member of the human race have become special testimonies in our churches. God's word teaches that our heavenly Father shines and rains on the just and the unjust. (Matthew 5:45) This means regardless of your belief, race, gender or background, there are certain things you are entitled to enjoy in life because you are a human being. When we lose focus on what Jesus came to do, we shallowly lower the standard for a bunch of lifeless and legalistic hyperboles. Is it not a concern today that it is possible to attend an average church where Jesus and His finished work of grace is barely mentioned or even completely swept into oblivion. Every good thing has come into the center stage except Jesus the only true gospel. Miracles, healings, prosperity, deliverance, nation building, charity, successful living, prayers, signs and wonders etc. are more prominent than Jesus Himself. It looks to me that Jesus is in a hurry to take over His church back from the religious wingnuts and gladiators.

The point is, anything else apart from Jesus is not sustainable. It is boring, tiring and nauseating. That is why people get emasculated and worn out. A life without Jesus is a laborious and self-improvement journey, which when push comes to shove, makes us pigeonholed in a wasteland of dead religion devoid of true joy and peace.

The word of God comes alive and refreshing when we ask the Holy Spirit to reveal Jesus to us in all the pages of the Holy Bible. As we shall see later in this book, the whole creation and all humans will fall apart without Jesus. His influence and His work of grace is what is keeping the entire human race together. There is no life without Him. For in Him we live and move and have our being. (Acts 17:28) There is no Bible without Him. There are no patriarchs without Jesus. Prophets, priests and Kings are irrelevant without Him. They all existed because of Him. Adam and Eve came into existence because of Jesus. Nations, discoveries, inventions, creativities, civilizations etc. exist because of Him. Jesus Christ is not an addendum. He is the real deal.

# *Chapter Four*

*It can't be Jesus
plus something else.*

## The Only Gospel:
# JESUS PLUS NOTHING

CHAPTER
**FOUR**

## The Only Gospel:
# JESUS PLUS NOTHING

Tthe gospel is the good news about what Jesus Christ has done. The gospel is not the unfinished but the finished work of Jesus. The gospel is the death, burial, resurrection and ascension of the Lord Jesus Christ for our justification by faith.

The Greek word for the gospel is *"evangelion"* which means good news. In fact, in the original text, it is described as something too good to be true. We are instructed to preach the gospel of the kingdom which some have concluded is different from the gospel of grace.

Now if the gospel is good news, then the gospel of the kingdom will be the good news of Jesus Christ. Got it? Some even say that Jesus' message of the kingdom is the original message while the gospel of grace is Apostle Paul's message and that grace preachers elevate Paul's revelation above that of Jesus. The truth is, the reverse is the case. Every true teacher or preacher of the gospel actually takes the word of Jesus more seriously. It's just that we must learn to study God's word (Jesus' word) in context. We must be diligent in our study to know what Jesus said, when He said it, to whom did He say what He said and for what reason. If we don't do these, we might be taking somebody else's medication for a different illness.

It is therefore a fatal incongruence to think that apostle Paul and the other apostles preached a different message from what Jesus commanded us to preach. That will be like a house divided against itself that cannot stand. If the claim that apostle Paul preached another gospel was true, then we are in a serious rancorous travesty because he wrote two third of the epistles. The blatant truth is that all the apostles including Peter, John, James, Jude and the others all preached Jesus Christ and His finished work of grace alone. Their styles may be different, but the gospel of grace is the core of their message. No one can go wrong by preaching Jesus and His finished work. The fear that percolates the very foundation of this liberating message will be unnecessary if we trust God that He is eternally smarter than all of us when He sent His son to die for our sins.

In the subsequent chapters, we shall examine the ubiquitous presence of Jesus Christ in the entire Bible from the beginning to the end. Ironically, if you have been a Christian for a few years and you ask an average preacher to describe his calling or the message he has been sent to preach, you will likely hear things like, "My message is deliverance." Others will say prayer, purpose, holiness, prosperity, victory and other great adjectives describing the main thrust of their ministries. While nothing is wrong with those great things in themselves and the good intentions to help people, but a closer look at the context of our theology will reveal a foundational flaw. I believe a great number of men and women of God have a great desire to help people, but clarity of basic theology cannot be swept under the carpet. It is a matter of life and death.

If we refuse to do a theological reevaluation of what we believe, we might be sincerely leading a whole generation into a convoluted understanding of God that will always produce a self-salvation scheme. Our theology must be rooted and grounded on Christ alone. He is the only message to preach. It is unfortunate that we have made the imperatives (the benefits of the message), *the message*.

For instance, deliverance, love, holiness, purpose, success, healing, prosperity, prayer, eschatology and the rest of what our ministries preach today are supposed to be by-products of the message of Jesus Christ and His finished work of grace. Jesus/Grace is the root while the other great messages are the fruits. Jesus is the hub that is holding all the wheels. Because Jesus is grace and grace is Jesus (John 1:17), it is safe to say that we cannot effectively do any of the imperatives without grace. Show me a man or a woman who can walk in true agape love without the grace of God. Who can pray effectively without God's grace? The man who can live holy in a perfect way without God's grace is not yet born. "Deliverance ministry, miracle ministry, healing, purpose" and the other things we have made the message are not the message but the manifestations of the message. Acts 8:5 emphatically states, *"Then Philip went down to the city of Samaria, and preached Christ to them"*. These are the words or phrases that are contextually used interchangeably with the phrase "preached Christ."

They are:

*Kingdom of God* Matthew 24:18-20

*The Word of faith* Romans 10:8

*The Gospel of Salvation* Romans 1:13-14, 1 Peter 1:10-12 Jude 3.

*The Word of Grace* Acts 20:32

*The Word of Life* 1John 1:1-4

*The Gospel of God* Romans 1:1

*The Gospel of Christ* Romans 1:16, Romans 10:16, Mark 16:15, 1Corinthians 15:1

*The Gospel* Acts 2:22, 3:13, 4:2, 5:27, 42, 8:5, 25, 9:20, 10:38-43, 11:20, 17:1-3,16-18, 18:5, 24-27

*The Gospel of the Kingdom and Christ* Acts 19:8-14, 20:17-24, 28:2-3, 31.

## The True Gospel

Our world has witnessed and still experiencing three main thrusts of doctrinal frameworks. Without going to the complex analysis of each of them in this chapter, they are: Pure legalism, Mixed grace (grace plus legalism) and Pure grace.

Basically, all the four main religions today practice legalism which is essentially a do-it-yourself, self-focused, self-serving ritualistic worship and ceremonies in an attempt to please God. Buddhism, Judaism, Hinduism and Islam all believe that you do good to get good from God and vice versa. Even the law of Karma teaches the same concept.

For the Christians and those who still want to practice pure legalism, the emphasis is on the Mosaic laws upon which the old covenant is premised. Unfortunately, nobody is even obedient to all the old covenant laws today. And James 2:10 says, *"If you obey every law except one, you are still guilty of breaking them all"* (CEV). In any case there are over 613 of them in all. Not just the Ten Commandments.

Because of our failures to keep all the Mosaic laws to the letter, we have ignorantly devised a way to be in the middle by picking and choosing which ones to keep and which ones to ignore and mixing the ones we think we can keep with the new covenant teachings. This is called mixture or mixed graced gospel. It is actually more dangerous than pure legalism because we are neither cold nor hot. It's either we cling to the law or to grace. There is no middle ground. It can't be Jesus plus something else. The word of God clearly states that if the old covenant had been faultless, there wouldn't have been a need for a new one. Ishmael and Isaac (law and grace) cannot be under the same roof. The former has to be cast out for the latter to inherit the promise (Genesis 21:10, Galatians 4:20). *A little leaven leavens the whole lump.* (Galatians 5:9) We should stop serving a healthy food mixed with poison or else we kill people. And people are actually dying spiritually when they are served with what the Bible calls dead preaching. (1Corinthians 3:17) Many of our modern-day churches fall into this

CHRISTOCENTRIC: THE ONLY GOSPEL

category of mixed grace preaching. I certainly believe that we have good intentions. It's just that we are sincerely wrong because of a faulty theological foundation. Like I mentioned earlier, the world has experienced different emphases that some have labeled movements. Examples of such movements are the holiness movement, prayer movement, faith movement, motivation movement, etc. Therefore, some have concluded that grace is also a movement that will soon fade away.

> Again, we run into error when we examine the message of grace independent of Jesus Christ. The two are intertwined. They cannot be separated. Remove Jesus from grace teaching and the message becomes hollow and a grotesque illusion.

First of all, grace is not a movement. A movement has a starting point and a terminal end. Grace on the other hand is a person. His name is Jesus. Can Jesus fade away? No way. Hebrews 13:8 says, *"Jesus Christ is the same yesterday, today, and forever."* Again, we run into error when we examine the message of grace independent of Jesus Christ. The two are intertwined. They cannot be separated. Remove Jesus from grace teaching and the message becomes hollow and a grotesque illusion.

The truth, is when Jesus and His finished work of grace is preached, all the other fruits of grace like holiness, prayer, deliverance, miracles, success etc. that have been labeled movements will no longer be things that are passing away but constant realities of the work of grace in our world.

# Chapter Five

> *Jesus is the only reason why an average human being, regardless of his or her race, religion or gender has the innate capacity to feel and experience realities of the celestial world.*

## Jesus and Grace in the Entire Cosmos:
# THE UBIQUITOUS NATURE OF JESUS

CHAPTER
**FIVE**

Jesus and Grace in the Entire Cosmos:
# THE UBIQUITOUS NATURE
# OF JESUS

Jesus Christ, no doubt is the most audacious man in history when you look at the tenacity in some of His statements regarding His Father, the Holy Spirit, Himself, His incarnations and the eternal purpose of the Trinitarian shared life with us. Even though, He was the humblest man that has ever lived, the candor in His Holy Spirit inspired declarations pierced through the heart like a double edged sword giving grace to the hopeless, emptiness to the religiously proud because He spoke the same message with two punchlines.

The gospel of John is more revealing to the incarnational ministry of Jesus working in absolute dependence on the Father and the Spirit to bring man back into *perichoresis*. After healing the crippled man who had never walked in John chapter 5, He reveals the loving nature of the Father *"... my Father works until now and I work..."* (John 5:17).

He goes on to say, *"the Son can do nothing of Himself but He does what the Father does"*. These statements are direct indictments on the mindset that suggests that the loving Jesus has come to rescue us from the hand of an angry God, as if to say that Jesus and the Father are separate. This idea that Jesus' main reason for existence was to settle the fight between us and God has unconsciously created the picture of a distant God who is constantly angry, but for Jesus' intervention.

It's the height of absurdity to imply that God is angry and Jesus is peaceful. God is smiting people with diseases from heaven and Jesus is healing them on earth through the Holy Spirit. God is killing people from heaven and Jesus is raising them from the dead. The Father is starving people with hunger and the Son is feeding them in their thousands. The Father is shouting hate and war but Jesus and the Holy Spirit on earth are spreading love and peace. It's like God is sending people to hell while Jesus is standing by the gate of hell to stop them from entering. If these were the case, then there is cacophony in the dance of the Trinity. The truth is, the Son and the Holy Spirit will never be at variance with the Father. They are consistently and forever in harmony with their rescue mission of lost humanity. The knee jerk response to this type of theology is an emotional blackmail against a loving God who loves us absolutely and for eternity. Most of these legalistic views of our heavenly Father that Jesus came to destroy are wrapped up in antiquated ambiguities. While focusing on the centrality of His mission as the Chief Executor of the Trinitarian eternal plan, Jesus made one of the most profound statements in all of eternity when He says in John 5:39, *"... the scriptures are all about me..."* (paraphrased). This statement did not go down well with the religious leaders of His days because to them, that was arrogance. But Jesus will not back down. In fact, He told them that they have mistakenly deluded themselves in thinking that they could find life by just searching the scriptures. Searching the scriptures is only as good if only we will find Jesus in the scriptures.

It is imperative to know that as at the time Jesus made this statement, the scriptures He was referring to are the Scriptures of the old covenant because there was no Mathew, Mark, Luke, John, Acts, and the epistles then. What are the scriptures He was referring to? Luke chapter 24 tells us. After His resurrection from the dead, Jesus did a series of revelatory message on the centrality of His person and the gospel of grace (death, burial, resurrection) to Cleopas and his friend who were depressed on their way to a village called Emmaus. He says, *"... 'O foolish ones, and slow of heart to believe in all that the prophets have spoken! Ought not the Christ to have suffered these things and to enter into His glory?' And beginning at Moses and all the Prophets, He expounded to them in all the Scriptures the things concerning Himself."* (Luke 24:25-27). "Moses and all the prophets" here refer to the books written by Moses which most Bible scholars and theologians agree are Genesis, Exodus, Leviticus, Numbers and Deuteronomy (the Pentateuch) or the first five books of the Bible. And the "prophets" here will mean all the other books of the old testament apart from psalms. At the end of the trip to Emmaus, where the other disciples were gathered, Jesus emphasized the pre-eminence of His person in the overall plan of the ages by also adding His place in the book of psalms as well.

> *"Then He said to them, 'These are the words which I spoke to you while I was still with you, that all things must be fulfilled which were written in the Law of Moses and the Prophets and the Psalms concerning Me.' And He opened their understanding, that they might comprehend the Scriptures. Then He said to them, 'Thus it is written, and thus it was necessary for the Christ to suffer and to rise from the dead the third day, and that repentance and remission of sins should be preached in His name to all nations, beginning at Jerusalem.'"* (Luke 24: 44-47)

Notice He says, *"... concerning me"*. This is very crucial. Why? It is because there are other things in the Old Testament scriptures that are good principles of life, beautiful stories, philosophies and wise proverbs but they are not as important as the person of Jesus and His work of grace. I mentioned earlier, every other thing in scriptures is only great to the degree that they reveal the preeminence of Jesus. One of the unkindest accusations that has been leveled against grace preachers and authors is to label them antinomian, a term used to describe anyone with the notion that moral laws or old testament scriptures have no basis under the gospel of grace. This is further from the truth for any true grace preacher because Jesus can be found in every book of the old testament through the help of the Holy Spirit as we will soon find out. Let's check out some scriptures that talk about the all-pervasive person and fullness of Jesus in the entire cosmos beginning with the 'I am' statement.

*"Then Jesus spoke to them again, saying, "I am the light of the world. He who follows Me shall not walk in darkness, but have the light of life." John 9:55: "As long as I am in the world, I am the light of the world."* (John 8:12).

Notice that He did not say "I am the light of the church or the light of the Christians". He says, *"I am the light of the world"* (I light the cosmos – I am responsible for all the good things of this world including civilization).

John 6:35-48 *"I am THE Bread of life."* Again, He did not say, "I am the bread of the church or the bread of the Christians". But He did say, *"I am the Bread of life"*.

John 14:6 *"I am THE Way, the Truth and the Life…"* Again, this is an absolute statement about Him regarding His assignment to the whole world through the Father and the Spirit.

John 15: 1-5 *"I am THE True Vine…"*

John 11:25 *"I am THE resurrection and the life"*

John 10:11-14 *"I am THE good shepherd"*

John 10:7 *"I am THE gate"*

Is'nt it amazing that the article "THE" is used in all the seven "I am" statements of Jesus to describe Himself and His mission as against the proposition "a"? He could have said, I am a door, I am a vine, I am a light, I am a gate, I am a resurrection and a life, I am a way, a truth and a life. I am a bread. Using the definitive article "the" to describe Himself as opposed to "a" simply means that there is no alternative. He is all-in-all in the Father and the Spirit.

It is still a mystery how we missed this in the modern church. We have removed the only gospel that should be sacrosanct and have replaced it with mundane ephemeral bling-bling. No wonder we are always thirsty for those things that have replaced Jesus because 'He that drinks of "this water" (any other thing apart from eternal life) will thirst again. (John 4:13) Man's needs will forever be insatiable outside of Jesus no matter what we have. They will never be enough. The beautiful thing is that when we have Him we have everything because He owns everything.

John 1:3 says, *"... All things were made through Him, and without Him nothing was made that was made."* There was nothing that was created without Him. That includes everything in eternity past, present and future. Because with God, there is no time. He lives in eternity and eternity lives in Him.

Colossians 1:12 says, *"giving thanks to the Father who has qualified us* (past tense) *to be partakers of the inheritance of the saints in the light."* The inheritance of the believers in Christ is already guaranteed in God. Romans 8:32 says, *"He who did not spare His own Son, but delivered Him up for us all, how shall He not with Him also freely give us all things?"*

The overwhelming influence of Jesus is further corroborated in Colossians 1:15-18, *"He is the image of the invisible God, the firstborn over all creation.For by Him all things were created that are in heaven and that are on earth, visible and invisible, whether thrones or dominions or principalities or powers. All things were created through Him and for Him. And He is before all things, and in Him all things consist. And He is the head of the body, the church, who is the beginning, the firstborn from the dead, that in all things He may have the preeminence."* In other words, nothing exists without Jesus. These include visible and invisible things. Matter, mass, galaxies, seas, world inventions, creativities, animate and inanimate, tangible and intangible, the seen and the unseen realms. The entire cosmic realities including modern civilizations will disintegrate into nothingness without Jesus. *"...And He is before all things and in Him all things consist"*. Another translation says *"... all things hold together..."*, which means if it were possible to take away Jesus and the Trinitarian vision from the planet, all creations and in deed, all humans will lapse into non-beings. Everything will disappear into a gloomy darkness in microseconds. This revelation makes the gospel more exciting. What the world needs is not an opium or a lifeboat gospel but that Jesus Christ has already received the whole world unto Himself and the only thing left to do is believe. Not that our belief will make it happen because it has already happened, but our belief will enable us appropriate and enjoy what Jesus has already done. Telling the world that God has nothing against them because they have been reconciled to God is the true meaning of authentic Christianity.

This glorious gospel is better understood when it is studied from the gospel of John through Acts of the Apostles, the Epistles and all the scriptures referring to Jesus in the entire Bible. The book of John unveils the pre-incarnation of the Son of God, His incarnational manifestation, works, death, burial, resurrection and their significance to all mankind.

> *"In the beginning was the Word, and the Word was with God, and the Word was God. He was in the beginning with God. All things were made through Him, and without Him nothing was made that was made. In Him was life, and the life was the light of men."* (John 1:1-4).

John, the beloved, through the help of the Holy Spirit also unpacked the ageless oneness and unity between the Father, the Son, and the Spirit, and the centrality of Jesus in the whole scheme of things. *"…And the Word was with God…"* In the original Greek, it is translated *"…And Jesus was face to face with God"*, which means, they were in irreversible harmony. Jesus was in the beginning with God and all things were made through Him and nothing was made without Him. Not only that, the light in Him was the light of men (not the light of Christians alone). And this light conquers and eliminates darkness.

Jesus is the only reason why an average human being, regardless of his or her race, religion or gender has the innate capacity to feel and experience realities of the celestial world. It is still a puzzle that such an inerrant person is becoming so obscure in a world created through

Him and for Him simply because we are all trying to be politically correct, and in the process, compromise the truth of the gospel. This political correctness is a subtle trade-off attempt to preserve our empires. Not being bold to declare the lordship of Jesus in the different kingdoms of this world is an indictment of noble Christianity.

The certainty and the reality of the person and the work of Christ and our being included in God's plan should never be a trivial concept or mere assumption. It is the nucleus of the heart and soul of true gospel.

If you don't read this book in context and through the help of the Holy Spirit, you may erroneously think that Jesus is being exalted above the Father and the Spirit. That will be a misunderstanding. This book is actually about the Trinitarian vision in ageless eternity past. But, Jesus the Son became the Executor-in-chief, working in unity with the Father and the Spirit. John 5:26. *"...For as the Father has life in Himself, so He has granted the Son to have life in Himself, and has given Him authority to execute...".*

John, the beloved, through the help of the Holy Spirit also unpacked the ageless oneness and unity between the Father, the Son, and the Spirit, and the centrality of Jesus in the whole scheme of things. *"...And the Word was with God..."* In the original Greek, it is translated *"...And Jesus was face to face with God"*, which means, they were in irreversible harmony.

This unity within the Trinity runs through the earthly ministry of Jesus Christ. To the Holy Spirit, He says, *"...The Spirit of the Lord is upon* me..." Luke 4:18 (The Spirit of God is upon Jesus. You see the three of them again). Acts 10:38 *"...How God anointed Jesus of Nazareth with the Holy Spirit..."* (God, Jesus and the Holy Spirit). At the water baptism of Jesus, the Holy Spirit, like a dove, came on Jesus and the Father spoke from heaven to endorse Jesus' sonship and ministry. *"...This is my beloved Son in whom I am well pleased".* Can you see the synergy?

> Referring to the Father, Jesus will say things like, *"...My food is to do the will of Him who sent me and to finish His work"* (John 4:34)
>
> *"My Father has been working until now and I have been working"* (John 5:17)
>
> *"Most assuredly, ...the Son can do nothing of Himself but what He sees the Father do. For whatever He does, the Son also does in like manner. For the Father loves the Son and shows Him all things that He Himself does..."* (John 5:19-20).
>
> *"...And the Father Himself, who sent me has testified of me..."* (John 5:37).
>
> *"I have come in my Father's name..."* (John 5:43).
>
> *"...This is the work of God, that you believe in Him whom He sent"* (John 6:29).
>
> *"...All that the Father gives me will come to*

*me, and the one who comes to me I will no means cast out. For I have come from heaven, not to do my own but the will of Him* (Father) *who sent me"* (John 6:37-38).

*"No one come to me unless the Father who sent me draws him, and I will raise him up at the last day"* (John 6:44).

*"...As the living Father sent me and I live because of the Father, so he who feeds on me will live because of me"* (John 6:57).

*"...I have said to you that no one can come to me unless it has been granted to him by my Father"* (John 6:65).

*"My doctrine is not mine..."* (John 7:16-18).

*"...I am not alone, but I am with the Father who sent me..."* (John 8:16).

*"...The Father has not left me alone for I always do those things that please Him..."* (John 8:29)

*"...Most assuredly, I say to you, before Abraham was, I AM"* (John 8:58).

*"...I must work the works of Him who sent me..."* (John 9:4-5).

*"...My sheep hear..."* (John 10:27-30).

At the tomb of Lazarus, Jesus prayed *"...Father, I thank you..."* (John 11:42).

*"...He who has seen me has seen the Father..."* (John 14:9-11).

*"...Father, the hour has come..."* (John 17:1-5).

## Jesus' Harmony with the Holy Spirit

Study with me the following testimonies of Jesus concerning His relationship with and the influence of the Holy Spirit in His own ministry.

> *"And I will pray the Father, and He will give you another Helper, that He may abide with you forever— the Spirit of truth, whom the world cannot receive, because it neither sees Him nor knows Him; but you know Him, for He dwells with you and will be in you. I will not leave you orphans; I will come to you."* (John 14:16-18).

> *"But when the Helper comes, whom I shall send to you from the Father, the Spirit of truth who proceeds from the Father, He will testify of Me. And you also will bear witness, because you have been with Me from the beginning."* (John 15:26-27).

> *"But now I go away to Him who sent Me, and none of you asks Me, 'Where are You going?' But because I have said these things to you, sorrow has filled your heart. Nevertheless I tell you the truth. It is to your advantage that I go away; for if I do not go away, the Helper will*

*not come to you; but if I depart, I will send Him to you. And when He has come, He will convict the world of sin, and of righteousness, and of judgment: of sin, because they do not believe in Me; of righteousness, because I go to My Father and you see Me no more; of judgment, because the ruler of this world is judged. I still have many things to say to you, but you cannot bear them now. However, when He, the Spirit of truth, has come, He will guide you into all truth; for He will not speak on His own authority, but whatever He hears He will speak; and He will tell you things to come. He will glorify Me, for He will take of what is Mine and declare it to you. All things that the Father has are Mine. Therefore I said that He will take of Mine and declare it to you."* (John 16:5-15).

*"The Spirit of the LORD is upon Me, Because He has anointed Me to preach the gospel to the poor; He has sent Me to heal the brokenhearted, To proclaim liberty to the captives, And recovery of sight to the blind, To set at liberty those who are oppressed; To proclaim the acceptable year of the LORD."* (Luke 4:18-19).

*"Then Jesus, being filled with the Holy Spirit, returned from the Jordan and was led by the Spirit into the wilderness..."* (Luke 4:1).

> *"How God anointed Jesus of Nazareth with the Holy Spirit and with power, who went about doing good and healing all who were oppressed by the devil, for God was with Him."* (Acts 10:38).

> *"But if the Spirit of Him who raised Jesus from the dead dwells in you, He who raised Christ from the dead will also give life to your mortal bodies through His Spirit who dwells in you."* (Romans 8:11)

The Spirit also came upon Jesus without measure. (John 4:24). I hope that it is clear that the collaboration between the Father, the Son and the Holy Spirit is not flippant. It is the core of the gospel message. The main theme of this book is: The Symphony of Love, embodied by the Trinity is being chiefly executed by the Son whom the Father has appointed to be the heir of all things.

# Chapter Six

Jesus is the thematic
truth of the scriptures.
*"...Was it not necessary for
the Christ to suffer these
things and enter into
His glory..."*
(Luke 24:26).

## Jesus in the Entire Bible:
# CHRISTOLOGY

CHAPTER
**SIX**

# Jesus in the Entire Bible:
# CHRISTOLOGY

As stated in the previous chapter, the Christological truth is the overall general thesis of the Bible. When the Bible says *"...And beginning from Moses to the prophets..."* Jesus expounded from the scriptures everything concerning Himself, He was referring to the entire 39 books of the old testament. "Moses" will be Genesis to Deuteronomy. And the "prophets will be from Joshua all the way to Malachi. He is the message of the Bible. With an open heart through the help of the Holy Spirit, a journey from the first book of the Bible to the last reveals Jesus in every book.

In Genesis, Jesus is the seed of the woman that would bruise the head of the serpent (devil) in His perfect finished work of redemption.

In Exodus, Jesus is the Passover lamb.

In Leviticus, Jesus is the High Priest.

In Numbers, Jesus is the pillar of cloud by day and a pillar of fire by night.

In Deuteronomy, Jesus is the Prophet like unto Moses.

In Joshua, Jesus is the Captain of our Salvation.

In Judges, Jesus is our Judge and Lawgiver.

In Ruth, Jesus is the Kinsman-Redeemer.

In I Samuel & II Samuel, Jesus is the Prophet of the Lord.

In I& II Kings, Jesus is the reigning King.

In I &II Chronicles, Jesus is the glorious temple.

In Ezra, Jesus is the faithful scribe.

In Nehemiah, Jesus is the rebuilder of the broken walls.

In Esther, Jesus is Mordecai.

In Job, Jesus is the Dayspring from on high.

In Psalms, Jesus is the Lord who is our Shepherd.

In Proverbs and Ecclesiastes, Jesus is the Wisdom of God.

In Song of Solomon, Jesus is the lover and the bridegroom.

In Isaiah, Jesus is the wonderful, counselor, mighty God and Everlasting Father.

In Jeremiah, Jesus is the weeping Prophet.

In Lamentation, Jesus is weeping Messiah.

In Ezekiel, Jesus is the river of life.

In Daniel, Jesus is the fourth man in the fiery furnace.

In Hosea, Jesus is the ever-faithful husband pursuing the unfaithful bride.

In Joel, Jesus is the Baptizer with the Holy Spirit.

In Amos, Jesus is the burden bearer.

In Obadiah, Jesus is the Mighty Savior.

In Jonah, Jesus is the forgiving God.

In Micah, Jesus is the Messenger with Beautiful feet.

In Nahum, Jesus is the avenger of God's elect.

In Habakkuk, Jesus is the Great Evangelist crying for revival.

In Zephaniah, Jesus is the great Reformer.

In Haggai, Jesus is the Cleansing Fountain.

In Zechariah, Jesus is Pierced Son.

In Malachi, Jesus is the Sun of Righteousness rising with healing in His wings.

In Matthew, Jesus is the Messiah.

In Mark, Jesus is the Miracle Worker.

In Luke, Jesus is the Son of Man.

In John, Jesus is Son of God.

In Acts of Apostles, Jesus is the Holy Spirit.

In Romans, Jesus is our justifier.

In I&II Corinthians, Jesus is the last Adam.

In Galatians, Jesus is our Redeemer from the curse of the Law.

In Ephesians, Jesus is the Christ of the unsearchable riches.

In Philippians, Jesus is the supplier of all our needs, according to His riches in glory.

In Colossians, Jesus is the fullness of the Godhead bodily.

In I&II Thessalonians, Jesus is the soon coming King.

In I&II Timothy, Jesus is the mediator between God and man.

In Titus, Jesus is the faithful Pastor.

In Philemon, Jesus is the friend, closer than a brother.

In Hebrews, Jesus is the Blood of the everlasting covenant.

In James, Jesus is the Great Physician.

In I&II Peter, Jesus is the Chief Shepherd.

In I, II, & III John, Jesus is our Everlasting Love.

In Jude, Jesus is the Lord our Savior.

In Revelation, Jesus is the King of kings and Lord of lords.

Therefore, *"...In all the scriptures"* (Luke 24:27) refers to Jesus in all these old testament scriptures." We see the Living God doing expository teaching on the written word.

It is interesting to know that the word "scripture" is derived from the Greek word "graphe" which means "sacred" The English word "graphics" is derived from "graphe" which has a connotative reference to the illustrative written word of God. *"All the prophets have spoken"* (Luke 24:25) means all the prophets under the old testament spoke in one language about Him. They never contradicted themselves in spite of their different backgrounds, dispensations and experiences. The unity, precision and accuracy of their message can only be supernatural.

> All the apostles especially Paul preached the whole gamut of the Trinitarian vision as being encapsulated in the Person and the finished work of Christ.

Jesus is the thematic truth of the scriptures. *"...Was it not necessary for the Christ to suffer these things and enter into His glory..."* (Luke 24:26). This means Jesus would suffer first before entering His glory. The entire message of the Bible is one finger pointing to the Lord Jesus Christ.

All the apostles especially Paul preached the whole gamut

of the Trinitarian vision as being encapsulated in the Person and the finished work of Christ. You may be asking: are we not supposed to preach other things? Yes, every other thing will only be relevant when they are taught with Jesus in focus. In fact, the ten areas of systematic theology are only important because of Him. For example, *soteriology,* the doctrine of salvation cannot be taught without Jesus *"...for there is no other name under heaven given among men by which we must be saved." ..."* (Acts 4:12)

*Pneumatology* – The study of the Holy Spirit is incomplete without Jesus because the Holy Spirit is the Spirit of Christ.

*Anthropology* - We are all made in the image of God in Christ.

*Bibliology* – He is the word of God in the entire Bible. The Bible is about Him.

*Angelology* – Angels are created by Him, for Him and they minister to Him.

*Ecclesiology* – He is the Head of the church.

*Christology* – He is the central heart of the gospel.

*Hamartiology* – The study of sin, its origin and effects both here and after. He came to destroy the power of sin.

*Eschatology* – He is the one coming again to rule forever.

*The central theology* – He is the image of the invisible God. No one knows the Father better than Him.

Apostle Paul taught all these branches of theology effectively yet He says, *"For I determined not to know anything among you except Jesus Christ and Him crucified."* (I Corinthians 2:2)

He was so passionate with Christology that he says, *"we preach Christ and Him crucified..."* (I Corinthians 1:23)

Acts 8:5 says, *"Philip preached Christ unto them."* Colossians 1:28 says, *"Him we preach...."* In other words, we preach the full counsel of God from Jesus point of view and His finished work of grace.

## Jesus in Names, Offerings and Events in the Old Testament

### Systematic Typology

Typology is the idea that persons (e.g. Isaac) and events (i.e. the temple rituals) can prefigure God's plan at a later stage to provide understanding for divine intent (i.e. The person and the finished work of Christ).

Without going into complex theological details of Christ's types and shadows in the old testament, most Bible scholars, historians and theologians believe that certain characters, events, and offerings represent Jesus. For example, a few of them will be Noah who was instructed to build an ark with which to save the world. Jesus is the builder and the ark of salvation for humanity to those that will believe in Him.

Isaac is a type of Jesus that will be slain for mankind's sins.

Joseph is another type of Jesus that will be betrayed by His brethren. Boaz is a type of Jesus.

There is also the pre-incarnational existence of Jesus. It is also called Christophany. It is a term used to describe the bodily and physical appearance of a deity.

Jesus appeared in the form of Melchizedek in Genesis chapter 14. Hebrews chapter 7 confirms him to be Jesus. Also, the angel of the Lord that appeared to Abraham in Genesis 18:1-13. He was the fourth man in the fiery furnace set up by the heathen King of Babylon (Nebuchadnezzar). He attested to the truth that *"...the face of the fourth man looks like the Son of God."* (Daniel 3:25)

## Offering

Apart from character typology and Christophany, we also see Christ in all the major five types of offering instituted under the old covenant. This also reveals the overriding centrality of the person of Jesus in the old testament scriptures. When He announced *"It is finished"* on the cross as stated in John 19:30, He used a language of merchants or commerce. The debt is fully paid. The Greek word is 'Tetelestai' which means the debt has been fully paid. In this context, the debt of sins and all the offerings for sins have been fully paid (Galatians 3:13-15). He paid all the debts with one offering covering all the other offerings (Hebrews. 10:12). He also fulfilled the law including all its types and shadows (Matthew 5:17).

*Trespass Offering:* Jesus is our trespass offering because this offering is a mandatory atonement for intentional or unintentional sin. It will always take care of the dos and don'ts of sin. It was instituted for the purpose of preventing the violation of persons and properties either God's or man's. The blood of the ram or lamb will cleanse the conscience of the trespasser after he has paid back the wrong party with the principal and the fifth part (20% addition). (Leviticus. 6:1-7.) We are all indebted to God knowingly or unknowingly. Jesus became the trespass offering. In forgiveness, Jesus assumed the debt of sin and paid it all (Leviticus 5:14).

*Peace Offering:* Jesus is our peace offering. This offering under the old testament focused on a voluntary act of worship using spotless and healthy animals and a variety of breads. This offering may be given for a blessing received from God or in advance for anticipated blessing. (Leviticus 7:11-34).

*Meal Offering:* Jesus is our meal offering. (Leviticus 2:1-16)

*Sin Offering:* Jesus is our sin offering. (Leviticus 4:1-5)

*Burnt Offering:* Jesus is our burnt offering. (Leviticus 6:8-13)

# Chapter Seven

*A promise of food to a hungry man is good news. A promise of money to a poor man is good news. A promise of success to a failure is good news. But none of these promises are the good news of the gospel until Jesus is preached. People can have all the good things of life without seeing or listening to Jesus.*

## These are not the Days of the Prophets:
# NO MIXTURE

CHAPTER
**SEVEN**

## These are not the Days of the Prophets:
# NO MIXTURE

Reading and studying the Bible in the context of the person of Jesus Christ and His finished work is the beginning of a massive shift in the way we see our heavenly Father for who He truly is. This revelation in turn begins to produce an efficient and productive life of purpose and meaning. But when we mix other things together with Jesus and His finished work of grace, what we have is a spiritual and schizophrenic generation that is dysfunctional mentally, spiritually and even physically.

In the story of the transfiguration experience, we see a diabolical attempt to rubbish the preeminence of the person of Jesus and his finished work of grace through a systematic introduction of syncretism, an amalgamation of different religious points of view or schools of thoughts. The problem with this kind of mindset that suggests that we can add a little law in our message is so dangerous that the Father had to interrupt Peter in order to dismantle this ominous move. It's like saying a little poison in a plate of rice cannot kill anyone. No one still in their right mind will eat any food that contains a little portion of poison. I wouldn't. *"A little leaven leavens the whole lump* (Galatians 5:9). *"…The little foxes that spoil the vine"* (Songs of Solomon 2:15). In some cases, small things or little things that are allowed to fester are the very things that destroy people at the end of the day. With this background, let us look at Matthew 7:1-9

*"Now after six days Jesus took Peter, James, and John his brother, led them up on a high mountain by themselves; and He was transfigured before them. His face shone like the sun, and His clothes became as white as the light. And behold, Moses and Elijah appeared to them, talking with Him. Then Peter answered and said to Jesus, 'Lord, it is good for us to be here; if You wish, let us make here three tabernacles: one for You, one for Moses, and one for Elijah.' While he was still speaking, behold, a bright cloud overshadowed them; and suddenly a voice came out of the cloud, saying, 'This is My Beloved Son, in whom I am well pleased. Hear Him!' And when the disciples heard it, they fell on their faces and were greatly afraid. But Jesus came and touched them and said, 'Arise, and do not be afraid.' When they had lifted up their eyes, they saw no one but Jesus only.Now as they came down from the mountain, Jesus commanded them, saying, 'Tell the vision to no one until the Son of Man is risen from the dead.'"*

Jesus takes Peter, James and John, three of His trusted disciples to a high mountain theologically known as the mountain of transfiguration. His face gets transformed with the brightness of the sun while His clothes become as bright as light. The disciples watch this spectacular experience in amazement, the heaven splits open and two most prominent figures under the old covenant, Moses and Elijah appear. Moses representing the law while Elijah representing the prophets. Peter gets carried away in the frenzy and suggests *"...Lord it is good for us to be here, if you wish, let us make here three tabernacles; one for you, one for Moses, and one for Elijah".*

But our heavenly Father is not done yet. While Peter is still talking, a bright cloud overshadows them. He interrupts Peter with one of the most profound statements every preacher or minister must always examine carefully, *"'...this is my beloved Son* (referring to Jesus) *in whom I am well pleased. Hear Him!' The disciples fall on their faces on hearing this in fear, but Jesus touches them and says 'Arise and do not be afraid'"* This story is filled with a lot of powerful truths when unpacked carefully and reverentially and could spark an awakening that will sweep across cultures, kingdoms, endeavors and across the planet.

The first question will be, why did Moses and Elijah appear to Jesus in that supernatural experience? You will recall that Jesus said He has not come to destroy the Law and the Prophet but to fulfill it. (Matthew 5:17) In other words, Moses (Law) and Elijah (prophet) have come to affirm His ministry. The law has to be fulfilled in its entirety by a sinless man. The prophet has to supervise or enforce the fulfillment of the law. Anytime Israel walked away or broke the law of God under the old covenant, the prophets were sent to execute judgement. The mountain of transfiguration was a spiritual place of mutual interconnection and contextual relevance of two covenants as it were. Without a proper understanding of one, the other remains a mystery

No grace preacher with a sound understanding of the ministry of Jesus will belittle the ministry of Moses and Elijah. But we can ignorantly take their relevance and prominence out of context and do what Peter suggested, "Let us build three tabernacles here, one for Moses, Elijah and you Jesus". Isn't that what we are doing today knowingly or unknowingly? We build our ministries around the spectacular not around Jesus and His finished work of grace. I believe that a lot of us are sincere just like Peter but we are just simply sincerely wrong. Luke's account of the same story regarding Peter's statement actually adds, *"... not knowing what he was saying."* Most teachings and preachings today are still centered around Moses and Elijah, and not Jesus. We hear more of Moses (law) and Elijah (prophet). Yet God said from heaven *"... This is my beloved son in whom I am well pleased, hear Him."* Another translation says *"This is my son whom I love; with him I am well pleased and delighted! Listen to Him.* (Amplified version).

Peter's ranting is understood, we do the same today. It logically looks unfair to just obliterate these two illustrious figures, the other old testament prominent people and everything they did. "C'mon, take a look at all the miracles of Moses, Joshua, Caleb, Abraham and all the prophets. God, you want us to forget about all these great people? You don't mean it, do you?" Peter representing many of us seems to be saying "we know Jesus is the only Savior and we know He is your Son but He alone cannot have the preeminence."

We may never know the other dangerous things that Peter was going to say before the Father interrupted him. Thank God He did, the forces of darkness were going to sandwich the ministry of Jesus between the law and the prophets. As long as we preach a mixture, Jesus plus other things, the enemy is not bothered. But the Father was emphatic, *"...Hear Him"*. NIV translation says *"...Listen to Him"*. He did not say hear them or listen to them (i.e. Moses and Elijah). Their ministry was over, their appearance on the mount was to submit to the authority of Jesus. After Jesus spoke those comforting words of grace to them *"...Arise, and do not be afraid"*, He lifted them up from the ground in love. The word of God says "… they saw no one but Jesus only". That was the same encounter that Paul had when he says, *"For I determined not to know anything among you except Jesus Christ and Him crucified."* (1Corinthians 2:2) He also prayed for the church of Ephesus that *"...your eyes of understanding be opened..."* (Ephesians 1:18).

The heartbeat of God today is for us to always see and listen to Jesus only. *"...They saw no one but Jesus only."* When we see Jesus we see the Father. Unfortunately, we seem to be seeing a lot of people and things today except Jesus. We see gigantic buildings. We see our spouses. We see a lot of good things which are not bad in themselves, but may we begin to see Jesus only like the disciples did.

We also hear good news today, we listen to a lot of good messages and a lot of life- changing principles. These are good news but we are not called to just preach good news. Our commission is to preach the good news of the gospel embodied in Jesus Christ and His work of grace.

A promise of food to a hungry man is good news. A promise of money to a poor man is good news. A promise of success to a failure is good news. But none of these promises are the good news of the gospel until Jesus is preached. People can have all the good things of life without seeing or listening to Jesus. There are millions of non-believers today in our world who have in abundance some of the things Christians are killing themselves to have. What the world needs is Jesus and the finished work of grace and all other things we are dying to have will follow by default. And even if we don't have them in excess on this side of heaven, Jesus is enough.

Because of lack of basic understanding of sound doctrine, many of us assume that since we are hearing a message loaded with scriptures, we are hearing the gospel. At this point, you should know that Jesus is the only message of the Bible. The law and the prophets exist because of Him.

*"God, who at various times and in various ways spoke in time past to the fathers by the prophets, has in these last days spoken to us by His Son, whom He has appointed heir of all things, through whom also He made the worlds; who being the brightness of His glory and the express image of His person, and upholding all things by the word of His power, when He had by Himself purged our sins, sat down at the right hand of the Majesty on high, having become so much better than the angels, as He has by inheritance obtained a more excellent name than they."* (Hebrew 1:1-4)

God is the same, He has not changed because He is the same consistently but His methodology can. That doesn't mean He is inconsistent. It's just that He works with us without destroying our unique identity and will. He doesn't want zombies or robots as children. Therefore, He was consistently unfolding his plan at every stage in different dispensations until it climaxed with Jesus in His incarnation.

Therefore, He is no longer speaking to us today by prophets (old covenant method in this context) but by His Son Jesus (the new covenant of grace). Of course, there are still people today operating in the prophetic. The ministry of the prophet is still valid under the new covenant (Ephesians 4:8), (1Corinthians 12:28) but every ministry gift is supposed to operate within the premise of the new covenant work of grace. No prophet today should operate outside of the finished work of the grace of our Lord Jesus Christ.

Also, what does it mean, when the word says, "He is speaking to us by His Son"? It doesn't mean that Jesus is the one preaching today all over the world. It simply just means that God wants the preachers to depend on the Holy Spirit to reveal Jesus so people can hear about Jesus through their pastors, man or woman of God. When Jesus and his finished work is being preached, then the Father is speaking to us in these last days by His Son. In other words, every revelation, teaching and preaching must be filtered within the ambit of the revelation of Jesus. This point can never be over stretched.

If my life and wellbeing depends on the favor of a powerful man, I will rather listen to His beloved son than his cherished servants especially if I am looking for something more reliable and authentic. The prophets of old were great but none of them was flawless. They occasionally in their humanity misrepresented the nature of God. Remember when one of the disciples threatened to call down fire from heaven to destroy some people just like Elijah did? (Luke 9:54) In other words, if Elijah, God's prophet did it, then it must be valid. Jesus responded by setting the record straight *"you don't have that kind of spirit, the son of man has not come to destroy men's life but to save it..."*. (Luke 9:55-56)

Abraham was great, but he made mistakes, Isaac was a great figure but committed blunders. Jacob was a phenomenon but had a lot of issues. All the major prophets shook their worlds, but they were not perfect in character. They were only justified by faith (Hebrews 11). But only our Savior and Lord, Jesus Christ says boldly *"The prince of this world came unto me and found nothing in me"* (John14:30). Wouldn't we rather focus on a flawless person?

He was not only born sinless, He remained sinless and became the high priest who could identify with our weaknesses especially the darkness of sin. He did it supernaturally without sinning otherwise the sacrifice will be contaminated.

*"For we do not have a High Priest who cannot sympathize with our weaknesses, but was in all points tempted as we are, yet without sin."* (Hebrew 4:15).

You may be asking, are we not going to get bored if we only preach or hear Jesus alone?  I am glad you asked. The answer is a capital NO. No sailor gets bored exploring the deep vast ocean. One of the reasons for boredom is our attempt to separate Christ from His creation. The redemption of Christ is directly connected to all creations and everything that exists. Remember Hebrews 1:1-2, *"God, who at various times and in various ways spoke in time past to the fathers by the prophets, has in these last days spoken to us by His Son, whom He has appointed heir of all things, through whom also He made the worlds..."*

When you see the water in the river, you are reminded that He is the living water. When you see food or you are hungry, you remember He is the bread of life. When you are confused in life's journey, you remember He is the way.

Even though, He used these natural images to describe Himself, they have far more reaching spiritual narratives that are life changing. The point is, when you think you know enough of Jesus, the Holy Spirit reveals another side of Him that you have never seen. Little wonder, Paul cries out for a deeper encounter when he says, *"...that I may know Him and the power of His resurrection, and the fellowship of His sufferings, being conformed to His death."* (Philippians 3:10). This was a man who wrote two third of the New Testament. Paul also tells about the mystery in Christ which has been hidden from ages and from generations, but are now being revealed to His saints. (Colossians 1:26). Like Peter on the mountain of transfiguration, because of our lack of understanding of God's hidden revelation of Christ that is transformative, we have erroneously assumed that the Jesus only gospel is not enough and we are adding other variations.

The subtle deception in this logical argument is that it is okay to preach Jesus plus other things as long as we preach them from the Bible. Second, it is okay as long as we preach characters that Jesus Himself affirms. Third, as long as our messages are morally sound then we are okay. Those three points are great, but they are not the gospel. If they are, then the three other major religions are preaching the gospel or at least are close to preaching it. All three major religions, Buddhism, Hinduism, Judaism and even certain sect of Islam preach moral character and decency. The moment we embrace this prototype, we just render the cross null and void. Paul says it better in Galatians 2:20-21, *"I have been crucified with Christ; it is no longer I who live, but Christ*

*lives in me; and the life which I now live in the flesh I live by
faith in the Son of God, who loved me and gave Himself for
me. I do not set aside the grace of God; for if righteousness
comes through the law, then Christ died in vain."*

A self-focused mentality indirectly says Jesus actually
didn't have to come, we could do better on our own. You see,
the true preaching of the Jesus centered message of grace is
very offensive to the religious ones. It's like telling them that
all your sacrificial righteousness before God is nonsense
and empty before Him. It can be very painful. I get it.
Especially, if it has taken us a lifetime of hard sacrifices to
build this legend of ourselves thinking we are holy because
of our discipline and stoicism. Discipline, sacrifice and
personal consecration to live a life that honors the Lord is
great and it is good for a structured social engagement in a
civil society. But it means nothing to God outside of the
cross. However, a life that has embraced the life of Jesus
whole heartedly will be supernaturally honoring to God.
And that, my friend, is far better than a moral lifestyle.

Notice also that Jesus told Peter, James and John not to
disclose their experience on the mountain to anyone until
He was risen from the dead. Why that instruction? It is
because what the Father said about listening only to Jesus
will only be officially valid after He had been offered up as
the eternal sacrifice and had risen from the dead. Peter
refers to this fabulous experience later in his epistles in a
way that suggests that the disciples finally got the message.
He is particular about what they heard versus their
spectacular experience. The supernatural and the
spectacular are important. By the grace of God, I can boldly

say that I constantly experience this in my ministry. But the person of Jesus and God's message of love is what drives the miraculous and not the other way around. The spectacular and the miraculous are a means to an end. Christ is the end in this context. 1 Peter 1:16-19 *"because it is written, 'Be holy, for I am holy.' And if you call on the Father, who without partiality judges according to each one's work, conduct yourselves throughout the time of your stay here in fear; knowing that you were not redeemed with corruptible things, like silver or gold, from your aimless conduct received by tradition from your fathers, but with the precious blood of Christ, as of a lamb without blemish and without spot."*

In other words, we saw Jesus in His majesty and glory. We saw the supernatural and the miraculous. But the Father just used it to get our attention to point us to something more serious and eternal. *"... And we heard this voice which came from heaven when we were with Him on the holy mountain. And so we have the prophetic word confirmed, which you do well to heed as a light that shines in a dark place..."*. The prophetic word which you do well to heed is what the Father said on that day, *"...This is my beloved son in whom I am well pleased, Hear Him."*

When we see and hear Jesus only, we become enamored with His glory and we are transformed into His image (II Corinthians 3:18). This brings us into a realm of conscious awareness of our joint-heir status with Christ. You don't bang your head on the chairs, punch the air or get involved in theatric drama to partake in what is already yours. No wonder, many God's children are tired, weak, frustrated and angry because we have lost focus of who and what to pursue (The revelation of Jesus Christ) while we are pursuing things that should pursue us. God did not spare anything. He gave us His all. *"He who did not spare His own Son, but delivered Him up for us all, how shall He not with Him also freely give us all things?"* (Romans 8.32)

# Chapter Eight

> *True greatness in God's kingdom can be summarized into one sentence: Embracing the love of Christ first for yourself and sharing it with others by pointing them to Jesus like John the Baptist did.*

## Losing your members to the Church of Jesus Christ:
## TRUE GREATNESS

## CHAPTER
# EIGHT

## Losing your members to the Church of Jesus Christ:
# TRUE GREATNESS

I n the exact words of Jesus Christ, John the Baptist was the greatest man that has ever lived (Matthew 11). That was an undaunted statement from the Son of God who can never lie. But the concluding part of those gracious words about John the Baptist is more interesting, *"…he that is least in the kingdom of God is greater than John the Baptist."* (Matthew 11:11)

Why will Jesus affirm John the Baptist as the greatest man that has ever lived on the face of the earth at the time? The implication of this statement is serious. It means that Abraham, the patriarchs, the prophets and the Kings, in spite of their greatness, are all not compare to John the Baptist. There could be many reasons why this is so. But the most outstanding among them is connected to John the Baptist's prophetic statement, where he declared his mission in relation to Jesus'.

*"In those days John the Baptist came preaching in the wilderness of Judea, and saying, "Repent, for the kingdom of heaven is at hand!" For this is he who was spoken of by the prophet Isaiah, saying: "The voice of one crying in the wilderness: 'Prepare the way of the Lord; Make His paths straight.'"* (Matthew 3:1-3)

We see in these scriptures that John is probably the most emphatic of all the prophets in his understanding of the relevance of the prophetic ministry of Jesus. All the other prophets prophesied as the Spirit of God gave them utterance regarding the ministry of Jesus. But many of them may not have fully understood what they were talking about. But John the Baptist not only prophesied, he saw his own prophecy come to pass in his lifetime. He even interpreted Isaiah's prophecy of the coming Messiah *"...Repent, for the Kingdom of heaven is at hand." For this is He who was spoken of by the prophet Isaiah saying, "The voice of one crying in the wilderness prepare the way of the Lord; Make His paths straight'"* (John 1:2) He was obviously referring to Jesus, to show us that the prophetic ministry of Isaiah is only relevant to the degree that He can show us the ministry of Jesus.

At the Baptism in Jordan river, John almost stopped Jesus from being baptized but He prevailed on him by telling Him that His baptism had a deeper connotation than what could be seen, *"...permit it to be so now for this it is fitting for us to fulfill all righteousness."* Remember Jesus came to fulfill all the laws and the prophets that no man can. Don't forget that the ministry of John the Baptist at this point in the history of the nation of Israel had become a phenomenon that even soldiers and wealthy people from everywhere were traveling from cities to go listen to a prophet preaching in the wilderness. Imagine this respected prophet pointing to somebody else as being greater. *"...I indeed baptize you with water unto repentance, but He who is coming after me is mightier than I whose sandals I am not worthy to carry. He will baptize you with the Holy Spirit and fire"*. (John 1:11)

John the Baptist not only endorsed the ministry of Jesus as it were, He also intentionally and deliberately minimized his own ministry and that of the other old covenant prophets by pointing all of humanity to Jesus. He says, ".... that He (Jesus) may increase that I may decrease." (John 3:30) This is

> John the Baptist not only endorsed the ministry of Jesus as it were, He also intentionally and deliberately minimized his own ministry and that of the other old covenant prophets by pointing all of humanity to Jesus.

not just referring to the person of Jesus but everything He embodies. It is significant to remember that John the Baptist, was the 'reigning preacher' at the time; the one that the press will want to interview and publish his stories in their newspapers and TV programs if he were to be alive today. With that level of success, he would have broken all records of social media followership. In it all, he kept on pointing people to Jesus. All his statements are mainly about his assignment to Jesus. He seemed to be saying to his audience, "I am only relevant because of Jesus". The word of God says, *"There was a man sent from God, whose name was John. This man came for a witness, to bear witness of*

LOSING YOUR MEMBERS TO THE CHURCH OF JESUS CHRIST

*the Light, that all through him might believe. He was not that Light, but was sent to bear witness of that Light. That was the true Light which gives light to every man coming into the world".* (John 1: 6-9).

God sent John the Baptist to bear the light of Jesus. He was not the light. None of the prophets was the light. They were light bearers. No preacher today is supposed to be in the center stage if we are truly preaching Jesus as the light. We are only the light of the world only to the extent that we shine the light of Jesus in this dark world.

In John 1:15, John cried out saying *"… This is He of whom I said 'He comes after me is prepared before me, for He was before me" "…He was before me"* refers to Jesus' ageless or timeless pre-incarnational existence.

It is so disturbing today that all the other prophets are even more popular than the one who introduced Jesus to the world. Perhaps because there are no recorded stories of his exploits. As long as Jesus remained the focus of his ministry John the baptist was fine. He did not even seek to be famous. Read his testimony:

> *"Now this is the testimony of John, when the Jews sent priests and Levites from Jerusalem to ask him, "Who are you?" He confessed, and did not deny, but confessed, "I am not the Christ." And they asked him, "What then? Are you Elijah?" He said, "I am not." "Are you the Prophet?" And he answered, "No." Then they said to him, "Who are you, that we may give an answer to those who sent us? What do you*

*say about yourself?" He said: "I am 'The voice of one crying in the wilderness: "Make straight the way of the Lord,"' as the prophet Isaiah said."* (John 1:19-23)

Even though He was one, He would not even accept the title of a prophet when they asked him *"...who are you, that we may give answer to those who sent us?"* His answers were the same. *"... I am the voice of one crying in the wilderness. Make straights the way of the Lord."* (John 1:22-23).

Sometimes, we may never appreciate certain stories except we can relate practically with the characters, the settings and the story line. I can imagine the enormous weight of the pressure on John the Baptist which could make any preacher crumble and fall into deceptions. The challenge facing the church today is not so much of the people starting well but the pressure is on finishing strong. John the Baptist was doggedly focused on the only message the other prophets also prophesied: Jesus' suffering, burial and resurrection. The fallen human nature wants to enjoy the accolades, encomiums, paraphernalia, and the limelight etc. And there is nothing wrong with accepting honor and God's blessing. There is nothing wrong with accepting privileges and respect because of what God is doing through us, but it is still our responsibility to attack the pressure of making our ministry 'the ministry' instead of Jesus. Jesus should remain who He is in our lives, ministries, churches, families and other endeavors.

Like I mentioned earlier, one of the unique parts of John the Baptist's ministry is that He did not only prophesy or announce the ministry of Jesus but unlike the other prophets, he also saw at least the beginning of its fulfillment. John 1:29 says, *"The next day John saw Jesus coming towards him, and said, "Behold the Lamb of God who takes away the sin of the world..."* His use of the word *"The Lamb of God"* is highly imperative. Don't forget that John was the last prophet under the old covenant. He was the transitional prophet who stood between the end of the old and the beginning of the manifestation of the new. He was familiar with all the animal sacrificial systems enacted by God from the killing of the innocent animal in the Garden of Eden to atone for the sin of Adam and Eve. An act undertaken by God Himself to foreshadow the ultimate sacrifice of Jesus on Calvary's cross,

Also, as a student of the Torah and the Prophets, John had been taught and raised under the Jewish system of atonement having seen his parents, Zachariah and Elizabeth observed these rituals week after week and year after year. But He also knew that these yearly animal sacrifices were only covering their sins for just one year at a time. Through the help of the Holy Spirit, He declared one of the most remarkable prophetic words of all ages, *"... Behold! The Lamb of God who takes away* (not who covers) *the sin of the world."* Jesus as a Lamb is not covering our sin but He has taken it away once and for all time. Hebrews 10:12 says, *"But this Man, after He had offered one sacrifice for sins forever, sat down at the right hand of God"*

It is of utmost importance to see that John was prophetically universal in his ministry when he says *".... Who takes away the sin of the world."* What a caution for those who think or insinuate directly or indirectly that they can monopolize Jesus because they see themselves as the gatekeepers of heaven and they can tell Jesus who should be admitted. Hilarious isn't it?

The point is, Jesus is for every member of the human race, with no exceptions. However, as with the other prophets who are inconsistent because they did not have the Holy Spirit in an ever-abiding presence like we do today, John almost caved in under the pressures of life, but was quick to make adjustment to go back in alignment with his core message. He began to doubt the fulfilment of his own prophetic ministry when he was faced with the terror and agony of death, even though he recognized Jesus as the Messiah. For instance, he says, *"...I saw the Spirit descending from heaven like a dove..."*

John 1:32-34, *"And John bore witness, saying, "I saw the Spirit descending from heaven like a dove, and He remained upon Him. I did not know Him, but He who sent me to baptize with water said to me, 'Upon whom you see the Spirit descending, and remaining on Him, this is He who baptizes with the Holy Spirit.' And I have seen and testified that this is the Son of God."* He had to depend on God who sent him as a witness to show him who Jesus was. This is a testament to the fact that the best of us could be distracted with deceptions. There is no better time to be humble. And I am not just talking about deceptive humility of outward appearance but a heart one that will elevate the ministry of Jesus above ours even if it will bring a temporary fading away of our empires or organizations. After all, Jesus said *"Anyone who will lose his life will gain it back."* (Matthew

16:25) It is high time pastors, preachers and all those who are called into ministry began to lose their members to the Church of Jesus Christ just like John the Baptist did.

In John 1:35-40, God's word says, *"Again, the next day, John stood with two of his disciples. And looking at Jesus as He walked, he said, "Behold the Lamb of God!" The two disciples heard him speak, and they followed Jesus. Then Jesus turned, and seeing them following, said to them, "What do you seek?" They said to Him, "Rabbi" (which is to say, when translated, Teacher), "where are You staying?" He said to them, "Come and see." They came and saw where He was staying, and remained with Him that day (now it was about the tenth hour). One of the two who heard John speak, and followed Him, was Andrew, Simon Peter's brother."*

This is a very interesting passage of scriptures with some hidden truths. The background to this is: Like I mentioned earlier, at this time in the nation's history, the ministry of John the Baptist had exploded. He was the most famous preacher, the most sought after, the most respected and the most revered. Imagine the scenario where a famous man of God is introducing the ministry of an unknown man of God who is just starting his ministry and the members of this popular man of God begin to desert him for the new preacher in town. That's like losing your members to another church. Right? That was exactly what happened in this story. The moment John said *"...Behold the Lamb of God,"* two of his disciples and others left him to follow Jesus. They even went to stay with Him the same day. As if that was not enough, they went back to their former preacher to invite the other disciples telling them "…we have found the Messiah (which is translated, the Christ).

If this happens today, the public perception will be that John the Baptist's ministry is finished. He will be regarded as a failure. All manners of insinuations will surface. Some will say, "The anointing has left the man." Oh, he is living in sin, that's why his church is falling apart."  Yet others will conclude it is because he's preaching heresy.

Honestly, nobody can say for sure what was likely going on in the mind of John. Maybe he was frustrated or perhaps he felt like a failure. In fact, he became confused at a particular season of his life when he was imprisoned for speaking the truth. He probably expected Jesus to use His Messianic power to rescue him, but Jesus did not show up. Imagine losing your members to a new preacher in town that you just formally endorsed and this new preacher will not even come to visit you in the days of trouble.

> *"And when John had heard in prison about the*
> *works of Christ, he sent two of his disciples and*
> *said to Him, 'Are You the Coming One, or do we*
> *look for another?'"* (Matthew 11:3)

John sent two of his disciples to go and double check if Jesus was indeed the Messiah. The pressures or challenges of life will always be used by the enemy to attack our revelation of Christ and our spiritual identity. This was a man who announced *"Behold the Lamb of God…"* , but he was now doubting Him. Jesus sent words back to him saying, *"Go and tell John the things which you hear and see; the blind see and the lame walk; the lepers are cleansed and the*

LOSING YOUR MEMBERS TO THE CHURCH OF JESUS CHRIST

*gospel preached to them."* In other words, these are the evidences of the Messianic ministry. John, go and check your prophetic periscope again and see the alignment of the prophecy with what you are now seeing, Jesus seemed to be saying. *"And blessed is he who is not offended because of me"* He Added. (Matthew 11:6). Jesus wanted John the Baptist to know that He is not a political Messiah because that will limit the scope of His ministry. He is The Savior of the whole world. And that cuts across all spheres.

But Jesus will neither ignore anyone pointing people to Him nor bring a depressing closure to the person's ministry. Regarding John, He says, *"Assuredly, I say to you, among those born of women there has not risen one greater than John the Baptist; but he who is least in the kingdom of heaven is greater than he."* (Matthew 11:11)

Jesus affirms that the greatness of John is second to none that has lived from Abraham till when He made the statement. Why? Ironically, anyone pointing people to Jesus will be lifted by the same Jesus. It may look like you are losing. It may look like you are becoming irrelevant, but the only One, who can promote says you are the greatest. *"And whoever exalts himself will be humbled, and he who humbles himself will be exalted."* (Matthew 23:12) The most profound success in life that anyone could have is the one that is coming from God Himself. And the most precious affirmation we can all hope for is the one coming from our heavenly Father.

I believe those precious and gracious words from Jesus to John settled the question of his identity for ever even in the face of martyrdom as it were. Pointing others to Jesus, by using any platform that God has given to each and every one of us, is the greatest thing we can experience. It should be a delight, whether you are in entertainment, politics, business, media or other spheres of influence, your objective is to use these mediums to show the world Jesus and His finished work of grace.

Jesus also says that *"...The least person in the Kingdom is greater than John the Baptist."* What a declaration! What this means is that, those who will receive the sacrifice of Jesus and embrace the gospel of grace will experience kingdom realities. It also means that a new covenant believer will be justified by faith. Everything Jesus will endure to fulfill all the laws, the sufferings, the pain and the agony that He will go through to secure that spotless righteousness will be credited to the account of the believer in the new covenant.

It's like doing nothing to receive everything that Jesus has done. The only thing to do is BELIEVE. When you believe in your heart that Jesus is who He says He is and that He died and rose again, you instantly get translated from the kingdom of darkness to the kingdom of light. Everything happens in an instant. Now, that is a miracle that the old covenant saints did not witness in their lifetime. In fact, John the Baptist, the light bearer himself, who witnessed the birth and the early part of Christ's ministry, did not witness the death, burial, and resurrection, which is the heart of the gospel. This makes the believers today unique in the sense that we are the generation that is witnessing the prophetic fulfillment of age long prophecies of the coming Messiah.

Little wonder then, that angels desire to experience what is happening now and what is the prophetic future of the church. I like the way apostle Paul puts it in Colossians 1:26. *"The mystery which has been hidden from ages and from generations but now has been revealed to His saints."* That is why we preach Him (Christ). This means we preach His person and His work of grace and nothing else. *".... To them God, willed to make known what are the riches of the glory of this mystery among the gentiles: which is Christ in you, the hope of glory, Him we preach warning every man and teaching every man in all wisdom there we may present every man perfect in Christ Jesus."* (Colossians 1:27-28).

The conclusion of this chapter hinges on one fundamental truth: True greatness in God's kingdom can be summarized into one sentence: Embracing the love of Christ first for yourself and sharing it with others by pointing them to Jesus like John the Baptist did. It is imperative that we remain steadfast in God's love for us first before we start bragging about our love for Him. It is being grounded in the love of God that will establish our love for Him. We cannot give what we don't have. Neither can we give what we have not received. John the beloved, in his epistle says it clearly, *"... In this is love, not that we loved God but that He loved us and sent His son to be the propitiation for our sins."* (1 John 4:10). God is the initiator of true love and we simply just respond. It is time to intentionally and deliberately embrace His love in the person of Jesus and His grace alone and then share with others. We can only share what we have received and embraced. *"We love Him because He first loved us."* (1 John 4:19)

# Chapter Nine

> *Empire building is monumentally small thinking. God doesn't want to be contained in an environment, churches, denominations, organizations etc. No matter how big they look, they are too small in comparison to God's global vison for humanity.*

## The Grace Made Generation:
# BABYLON IS CRUMBLING

CHAPTER
**NINE**

## The Grace Made Generation:
# BABYLON IS CRUMBLING

I t is not uncommon today to see and hear people who claim they are self-made. Our world is filled with great achievers and highly successful people who believe they are self-made. In fact, brick and mortar bookstores and online retailers have designated sections for self-made or self-help titles.

Well-crafted titles like "Self-made millionaires", "self-made mothers", "self-made entrepreneurs", etc. scream at you in average bookstores all over the country and around the world. While there is nothing inherently wrong in being hard working and relishing in one's achievements in life, I believe when a truth is overstretched beyond limit, it becomes subjective. I guess the underlying intention of these "self-made" people is to uphold the dignity of labor and self-reliance, but to use an absolute terminology to describe one's success in isolation can lead to self-aggrandizement and a sense of ungratefulness especially to our Creator and everyone He has moved to help us at certain points in life.

The truth is, nobody is really self-made. No one carried his or her own pregnancy. Your mom did. Even your mom needed the help of your dad to conceive you. Those who helped your mom during pregnancy indirectly helped you. The nurses, the doctors, those who probably paid the hospital bills including those who helped raise you all contributed to your success in life. An old African proverb says it takes a village to raise a child.

Everyone that did one thing or another during your formative years including your teachers, friends, associates and enemies have all added some value to your life. This sense of unhealthy independent mindset that has metamorphosed into selfish and turgid movement did not start with this present generation. It dates back to the beginning of time. It's as old as the Garden of Eden where the old ideology started historically. Our heavenly Father in council of the Trinitarian union created Adam and Eve for the sole purpose of relationship devoid of fear and anxiety. Adam and Eve had everything they needed without them yelling out or crying in desperation. This abundant life without struggle is the real definition of grace. Grace is having life in its fullness, especially when that life is supplied by somebody else. Unfortunately, Adam and Eve decided not to trust God anymore but self. Satan capitalized on that loophole in their lives and twisted God's love for them in order to seduce them away from true love into self-deception. Because God created everything to reproduce after itself, Adam began to reproduce a self-conscious and self-focused generation. One of the saddest scriptures in the Bible is Genesis 5: 1-4: *"This is the book of the genealogy of Adam. In the day that God created man, He made him in the likeness of God. He created them male and female, and blessed them and called them Mankind in the day they were created. And Adam lived one hundred and thirty years, and begot a son in his own likeness, after his image, and named him Seth. After he begot Seth, the days of Adam were eight hundred years; and he had sons and daughters."*

Going through the book of Genesis from the first chapter, Genesis 1: 26-29, *"...God said, let us* (The Trinitarian Life) *create man in our image and our likeness".*

According to Genesis chapter 2, God created man in His image and gave him dominion and prosperity that is activated by grace/rest (Man was supposed to work in rest) because the first day of work for man was God's resting day. You don't get tired when you work from rest. In the natural, people work then they rest. But in the realm of God's grace, people rest first, then they work.

Genesis chapter 3: Eve was deceived and she and her husband fell. The enemy made them look away from God, their source of true identity. They took a plunge into self-occupation, self-effort and self-centered independence. Legalism began.

Genesis chapter 4: Self-effort and selfishness got aggravated to the level of bitterness and hatred. Cain killed Abel his brother because of jealousy and envy. Genesis chapter 5: Legalistic reproductive system began. Adam began to reproduce a self-centered and self-effort minded generation. I mentioned earlier that one of the most tragic scriptures in the entire Bible is Genesis 5: 1-4. It is because when you compare Genesis chapter 2 with Genesis chapter 5 then you get the clear picture. Adam's first-generation children born after his sinful nature and distorted image of God were to be responsible for the reproduction of every member of the human race including the over seven billion people currently living on the planet. That's why the writer of psalms says *"... Behold, I was brought forth in iniquity, And in sin my mother conceived me...."* (Psalm 51:5). Fast forward. By the time you get to Genesis chapter 11, it has become so bad. The vision of the Tower of Babel was conceived. "Babel" actually means "confusion". That is where the word Babylon is derived from

It was the first generation of Adam after the fall into the deception of self that reproduced other generations that finally produced Seth. Seth also reproduced the generation after generation that eventually reproduced the builders of the Tower of Babel, a type of self-effort, self-promoting and self-satisfying bombastic generation. The Tower of Babel was the beginning of New Age and humanism. Read their vision statement in Genesis 11: 1-4:

*"Now the whole earth had one language and one speech. And it came to pass, as they journeyed from the east, that they found a plain in the land of Shinar, and they dwelt there. Then they said to one another, 'Come, let us make bricks and bake them thoroughly.' They had brick for stone,*

*and they had asphalt for mortar. And they said, 'Come, let us build ourselves a city, and a tower whose top is in the heavens; let us make a name for ourselves, lest we be scattered abroad over the face of the whole earth.'"*

A casual reading of this vision statement on the surface is harmless until we analyze it in the context of our discussion of whether we want to be self-made or grace-made. It's God's perfect will for His creatures especially His covenant people to have great names and be made in life. The methodology and the process of making us and giving us great names is what we should pay attention to. Trying to be self-made or struggling to make ourselves is what is responsible for narcissistic tendencies, self-absorption and empire building that leads to vanity. You see, a life without God's grace consciousness is soulishly torturous. Our heavenly Father wants to make us and give us names quicker than we think. But it must be done within the perimeter of His covenant of grace alone orchestrated in Jesus Christ.

After the collapse of the Tower of Babel Empire, God called an unknown poor Abraham. Abraham was from an idol worshiping background where his predecessors worshipped the elements. An unlikely person to be called by God. Right? That sounds like God.

1 Corinthians 1:26-30 says, *"For you see your calling, brethren, that not many wise according to the flesh, not many mighty, not many noble, are called. But God has chosen the foolish things of the world to put to shame*

*the wise, and God has chosen the weak things of the world to put to shame the things which are mighty; and the base things of the world and the things which are despised God has chosen, and the things which are not, to bring to nothing the things that are, that no flesh should glory in His presence."*

Don't forget that Abram as he was called at this time, apart from his idolatry background also hailed from a self-made generation that attempted to build the Tower of Babel in Genesis chapter 11. The very next chapter starts with God calling Abram to separate himself from that generation. Most of the time when God wants to do certain unique things in your life, He separates you from your environment. This can be scary, lonely and confusing sometimes but it's always peaceful and exciting. It is always a time of retraining where God begins to do a theological revolution, reimaging, repurposing, reconfiguring and a recalibrating of your entire mindset.

*" Now the Lord had said to Abram: 'Get out of your country, From your family And from your father's house, To a land that I will show you. I will make you a great nation; I will bless you and make your name great; And you shall be a blessing. I will bless those who bless you, And I will curse him who curses you; And in you all the families of the earth shall be blessed.'"* (Genesis 12: 1-3)

A contextual and analytical study of these verses reveals

three main things that Abram was told to disconnect from: His country, his kindred (family) and his father's house. It was like Abram had to be rebirthed as it were. This physical disconnection is not as important as the spiritual and the soulish ones. In other words, God seemed to be saying "you must go through a season of loneliness with me where I will reveal myself to you and show you things to come. But as long as you remain in that legalistic or do-it-yourself environment you were born and raised, it will be difficult to comprehend what I am about to reveal to you." These scriptures are exciting. It looks like God is the one doing everything for Abram. He called Abram. He promised him. He will bring the promises to pass by Himself. All Abram needed to do was to believe him.

Notice how many times God used the pronoun 'I' in those three verses. Because He is the self-sufficient God. *"...To a land that I will show you. I will make you a great nation; I will bless you and make your name great; And you shall be a blessing. I will bless those who bless you, And I will curse him who curses you; And in you all the families of the earth shall be blessed.'"* When you compare the pronoun "I" in these verses with the pronoun used by the builder of the tower of Babel in Genesis 11: 3-4, you will see the reason God had to ask Abram to separate himself from that generation.

> *"'Come, let us make bricks and bake them thoroughly... And they said, 'Come, let us build ourselves a city, and a tower whose top is in the heavens; let us make a name for ourselves, lest we be scattered'".* (Genesis

11:3-4)

Again, God is not against greatness or being made. He wants to do it for us. The builders of the Tower wanted to just build a city and a self-glorifying empire and remain there but God wanted more. He wanted nations to experience His glory. Empire building is monumentally small thinking. God doesn't want to be contained in an environment, churches, denominations, organizations etc. No matter how big they look, they are too small in comparison to God's global vison for humanity.

God called Abram away from that generation and started preaching the gospel of Jesus to him. *"... And in you all the families of the earth shall be blessed..."* (Genesis 12:3). Only Jesus Christ will make that happen at the appointed time through His death, burial and resurrection (the gospel of grace). Abraham believed and he became righteous from that day forward regardless of his mistakes in his humanity. (Galatians 3:6). Who preached the gospel to Abraham? God Himself of course. Again, the message to preach is the good news of the Gospel. Galatians 3:8, *"... And the scripture, foreseeing that God would justify the gentiles by faith, preached the gospel to Abraham beforehand, saying "in you all the nations shall be blessed".* So, we see here that the blessing on Abraham is not just material, but a spiritual one embodied in his seed, Jesus Christ. The gospel of Jesus therefore is the blessing here that will spread across the nations of the earth including the gentile nations.

Thousands of years later, Jesus who has always been with

BABYLON IS CRUMBLING: THE GRACE MADE GENERATION

the Father and who is the embodiment of grace would make a similar statement to Simon Peter and his brother, Andrew who were fishing on a particular day. *"Follow me, I will make you..."* Jesus spoke the language they could relate with as fishermen because catching fishes and growing their business was the most important thing to them at this time.

Our all wise heavenly Father is more interested in making us than we want. The self-made paradigm is always parochial and limiting. These brothers wanted to be made but Jesus wanted to make them extraordinary fishers – fishers of men. Your extra effort turns you from ordinary achievers to earthly success while grace makes you and turns you into a global ambassador of God's kingdom. That, my friend, is extraordinary and supernatural. From being unrecognized local fishermen, Jesus made them into world class success stories whose impacts will remain in the sands of time for eternity.

God is still turning failures into success today. He is transforming cowards into confident leaders. He is still making and turning ordinary, ignorant men and women into champions and giving them great names that they couldn't have imagined on their own through the grace of our Lord Jesus Christ. Are you self-made or grace- made? The latter is better.

# Chapter Ten

*Jesus came to model the perfect example of true leadership which is 'serve to lead' (servant leadership). He turned the table around when He said, "...the Son of Man did not come to be served, but to serve, and to give His life a ransom for many."*
(Matthew 20:28, Mark 10:45)

## The Collapse of the Religious Empire:
# THE COMING SPLINTER

# The Collapse of the Religious Empire:
# THE COMING SPLINTER

W hen the German philosopher, Karl Marx said, "…religion is the opium of the masses", little did he know that he was unconsciously saying something that is absolutely true even though he was being sarcastic and derogatory. It is interesting to see the sense of humor in God's universe and how He occasionally employs the agency of the most unlikely people to execute His divine agenda. Remember what Caiaphas, the high priest, said regarding Jesus atonement,

> "…And one of them, Caiaphas, being high priest that year, said to them, 'You know nothing at all, nor do you consider that it is expedient for us that one man should die for the people, and not that the whole nation should perish.' Now, this he did not say on his

*own authority, but being the high priest that year, he prophesied that Jesus would die for the nations and not for that nation only, but also that He would gather together in one the Children of God who were scattered abroad."*
(John 11:49-52)

God cannot be boxed into a corner. In His sovereignty, He could choose to work out His eternal plans for the good of humanity through any means or anybody. Bear in mind though that His sovereign acts are not reckless and are not detrimental to us. Neither does He toy with our lives like robots or zombies just to prove a point. To think that God kicks us around or messes with our emotions in a cold, wicked and selfish way while He stands aloof to enjoy our pain and later watch us grinding our teeth and crawling on our knees to ask for His mercy is the real definition of a dangerous religion. That is actually the opium that religion is selling every day. I am glad that Karl Max compares the word "religion" to opium. Thanks to God he did not say Jesus is the opium of the masses.

What is religion? In the context of our discussion in this chapter, religion is an organized set of rules, regulations and ordinances formulated by certain elite of an organization and are to be kept by everybody in that organization especially the followers. In addition, obedience to those rules and regulations are rewarded by "God" and disobedience is punished severely both here and thereafter.

Many other philosophers also believe that religion has

certain practical functions in the society that are similar to the function of opium in a sick or injured person. It reduces people's immediate suffering and provides them with pleasant illusions that give them the "strength" to carry on. The conclusion is that religion is harmful as it prevents people from seeing the class structure and oppression around them. Therefore, religion can prevent necessary revolution.

> Many of the world's famous religions all have a feudalistic system that produces structural class consciousness.

Many of the world's famous religions all have a feudalistic system that produces structural class consciousness. The revered leader of the organization who is perceived as a demigod sometimes has a cultic following that makes the followers live a less than a human life. The major cardinal essence of religion is the idea that whatever instructions you are given must be carried out without questions. Remember disobedience is punished by the deity.

Under oligarchic religious system, the leader who is usually charismatic is the attention of focus. That was why Jesus was resisted violently by the religious leaders of His day because Jesus came to disrupt the status quo. The whole cosmos and humanity have always been about the Trinitarian vision and not a few self-absorbed legalists.

Jesus came to model the perfect example of true leadership which is 'serve to lead' (servant leadership). He turned the table around when He said, "...the Son of Man did not come to be served, but to serve, and to give His life a ransom for *many."* (Matthew 20:28, Mark 10:45)

Religion is so deadly in so many ways. It kills innovations. It resists empowering changes. It is retrogressive, oppressive and barbaric. Thank God, true Christianity is not a religion. It is the very life of Jesus Christ. Jesus did not come to improve on any of the existing religions nor did He come to establish a new one. He dismantled the religious fabrics and introduced kingdom living. John 10:10 *"... I have come that you may have life, and have it more abundantly."* The life here ('Zoe' in the Greek) is the very essence of God. It is God's seed, His DNA as it were. That is more powerful than religion.

This life of God in a believer strengthens him in the journey of life. It is not an opium whose effects is transient and evasive. I wish somebody had told Mr. Max that he was right in his statement and assured him what he actually wanted was the true gospel of Jesus Christ. I believe the yearning in the soul of this man then was Jesus Christ. I submit that there are several millions of people today like Karl Max who are truly yearning for the true living water that can quench the thirst in their souls. Paul encountered similar philosophers in Athens who were worshipping the unknown gods. He turned their philosophy around through the grace of God and preached Christ to them using their superstitious ideology.

I strongly believe that our heavenly Father is in a hurry to sweep people into His kingdom including people who are afraid of religion. He is about to shake the nations. There will be a destruction of the dominant social system and current cultic following: a practice that takes away the focus from Jesus and puts it on a charismatic leader. These "powerful leaders" will go through a process of brokenness, either through revelation or hard knocks in the school of the spirit until Jesus becomes the center of focus.

# *Chapter Eleven*

*Most of the times, physical occurrences and natural events are direct manifestations of spiritual realities.*

# A Disruptive Awakening of the Spirit:
# ORGANIZED CHAOS

CHAPTER
**ELEVEN**

# ORGANIZED CHAOS:
## A Disruptive Awakening of the Spirit

Are you familiar with the old saying, "Change is the only thing that is permanent"? I bet you do. One thing that is constant is change. Positive changes are healthy and exciting. However, some changes that threaten our fundamental cultures and belief systems are scary and so we resist them to the detriment of a lasting and sustainable legacy. It is not uncommon these days to read or hear words like disruptive technology, disruptive innovations, disruptive thinking etc. Well, while the coinage may be new, the whole idea is as old as the Bible.

There is nothing new under the sun. No one can accurately be called an inventor of anything except God, the Ancient of Days Himself. We are only discovering or re-discovering things that have always been. For instance, the law of gravity and all the other laws existed before their discoverers ever existed.

In the same way, Jesus came here to disrupt a culture and dangerous legalistic philosophy that misrepresented the nature of His Father. And there was resistance. Even today, major corporations and businesses that fail to respect changes and progressive disruptions are disappearing and some have actually fizzled. Blockbuster, a home movie and video games rental services giant with over 9094 stores filed bankruptcy after collapsing because it could not transition into the disruptive digital model. A few years later, Netflix, a major giant in the digital movie space is now worth $8.8 billion.

Polaroid, a former giant in the camera industry, resisted a positive disruptive change and also paid for it. They filed for bankruptcy in 2001 and assets were purchased by a company in digital filming and cameras. Other huge names that went belly up because they were swimming against the tide of innovative changes include Toys "R" Us, Borders Bookstore, Pets.com, Tower Records, Compaq, Kodak, and the list goes on. In fact, the common cliché now in Silicon Valley is, "Innovate or die".

The relevance of the examples of these global giants is to underscore a point that most Christian leaders ignore. We are always talking about disruptive technology, disruptive innovations etc. without paying proper attention to disruptive awakening of the spirit. Most of the times, physical occurrences and natural events are direct manifestations of spiritual realities.

Some of these disruptive experiences in our world today are neither good nor bad in some cases. It all depends on the way we respond or react to them. For instance, we can either use social media to preach Christ or use them to pull ourselves down. We can either use the internet to spread humanitarian awareness or use it to engage in unethical activities. It is up to us. We can complain, resist these innovations or welcome them for a positive use. A taxi driver may complain all he wants, Uber continues to grow. Brick and mortal stores could either join the train of online retailing space, learn some things from the likes of Jeff Bezos or complain and become irrelevant.

For the church (the body of Christ), it is even more serious. The most pro-active step we can take is to align ourselves with the re-awakening of the Spirit. Instead of taking time to diligently and with an open-heart study this new awakening of the message of grace that is Christ-centered, many Christians, especially leaders are fighting it vehemently. It is understandable. That's what happens if our success in life is being defined by religion, or achievements especially if our sense of worth is directly or indirectly tied to our "ministry". This achievement is the only thing we have known for years. It can be very frightening. It is difficult to let go your lifeline when you are sinking. Letting it go threatens our existence to the very foundation. We don't have a life outside of our empires. That is what we are living for. We will resist anyone or anything that suggests we should let it go. We are ready to die fighting to defend it. Religion has even taught us that defending our empires means we are defending the gospel.

And it may look like that on the surface for the undiscerning. But we know that the fight is really about us because it looks like we will no longer be in control. Not been in control makes us helpless, fearful and vulnerable. Nobody wants that in the flesh. Those are the feelings I have when I am at the passenger's seat when my wife drives me occasionally. I want to be in control of the wheels. It is high time Jesus took His church back.

Another reason why we panic is because our "calling" is responsible for everything and anything we have become in life. The respect, honor, blessing, fame, spouses etc. are all tied to this one thing.

However, God always has better plans because He is smarter than all of us. He wants us to still enjoy life through the freedom that is found in Jesus. And the only true way to enjoying this true freedom is if we give this gospel of Jesus and His grace alone to a desperate humanity.

Fighting the message of grace is like Blockbuster fighting Netflix. In fact, it is like a helpless, tired, warrior fighting a compassionate ally that has come to help him in the battle field simply because he is not familiar with his style. That is waging war against your helper. God seems to be urgent in bringing Jesus back into the center stage. The Holy Spirit seems to be saying, "Enough of making me the focus. My main ministry is to glorify Jesus. Don't make it about me". (John 16:14)

Before the great shaking begins for this gospel revolution, I believe there will be an assemblage of remnant of believers and ministers who are tired of religion and they are honest about it. God will bring these people together in the Spirit from all walks of life. They will be saying the same thing like apostle Paul said, *"For I determined not to know anything among you except Jesus Christ and Him crucified."* (1 Corinthians 2:2). Our heavenly Father is calling those who are drowning in the sea of religion. I am not a swimmer. But I understand that a life saver trying to rescue a drowning man has two choices. Firstly, he waits until the perishing man gets tired after he has hopelessly tried to rescue himself. Secondly, if the life saver cannot wait, he jumps into the river, knocks out the drowning man's shoulders and knees so he becomes weak or else he will drown himself and the life saver in an attempt to rescue himself in desperation. What a powerful illustration. I believe God is either waiting for us to give up on our efforts to save ourselves when we get tired of trying or get knocked out with frustrations that will finally lead us to the place of grace. (Jesus Christ)

This place in Christ alone is the best environment to be - the safest place in the entire known and unknown world. The song writer is right when he says, "Rock of Ages, cleft for me. Let me hide myself in thee…" or better still, 'Let me live with and in thee'. Because with Christ, we are indivisibly united. Nothing in creation can ever separate us again. Glory be to God for ever more.

*"Who shall separate us from the love of Christ? Shall tribulation, or distress, or persecution, or famine, or nakedness, or peril, or sword? As it is written: "For Your sake we*

*are killed all day long; We are accounted as sheep for the slaughter."Yet in all these things we are more than conquerors through Him who loved us. For I am persuaded that neither death nor life, nor angels nor principalities nor powers, nor things present nor things to come,  nor height nor depth, nor any other created thing, shall be able to separate us from the love of God which is in Christ Jesus our Lord".* (Romans 8:37-39)

For some reasons, historically, our heavenly Father has always been on the side of the masses especially those who are being oppressed either by political leaders or religious slave drivers. After series of warnings, appeal, signs and prophetic visitations to get the attention of these rulers to let people enjoy freedom and they are recalcitrant, He allows their empires to go through shakings for the emancipation of the helpless. A lot of beautiful ancient empires have all come and gone with their emperors kissing the dust.

Without going into details, the Babylonian empire, Greek empire, Persian empire,  Egyptian empire,  Roman empire etc. at one time were cynosures of beauty and grandeur before they collapsed. Their fall hinges on three main fundamental flaws.

They all over-expanded. Dreaming big is great but not knowing the difference between vision and ambition could be a tragic flaw. Not every growth in a human body is healthy. So is it in life and ministry. Certain growths on the body are taken out surgically. What kind of food are we serving the crowd of people that are coming? Good news or the good news of the Gospel? Are we serving them foods of new age, humanism, legalism or even syncretism? Emperors don't care about the health of their people. They only care to the degree that the empire is stable and expanding. Everything starts and ends with the ruler.

> Dreaming big is great but not knowing the difference between vision and ambition could be a tragic flaw. Not every growth in a human body is healthy. So is it in the ministry.

Another crack that every fallen empire experiences before the final collapse is encroachment of enemy forces disguising as loyal troops. A church or ministry that is overly ambitious for growth regardless of the content of its message will not know when the "mix multitudes" invade the leadership structure. This is so dangerous that apostle Paul addressed it using strong words like, "who has bewitched you… Are you so foolish? Let anyone preaching another gospel be accursed." He was using these strong words to oppose the Judaizers, (a sect of legalistic Jewish teachers), who tried to corrupt the faith of the Galatian Church members. Paul had to remind these believers that they received Christ by faith and they will maintain and go with Christ by faith alone. (Galatians 1:6-9, 3:1-10) The only time any ministry gift is relevant is if they help establish you in the faith with Christ being the focus.

It is interesting to know that the early church had explosive numerical growth, but they were not going to allow sorcerers and dangerous men in their leadership. Peter sharply rebuked a man named Elymas for trying to merchandize the grace of God. You can't put a price tag on grace. *"May your money perish with you..."*, he says (Acts 8:20).

The glory of God was so heavy on the church that the seven sons of Sceva trying to fake the power of God were taught a lesson never to toy with sacred things. (Acts 19:11-20). Today, the church is almost becoming a laughing stock because of mixed multitudes, an encroachment of enemy forces disguising as loyal troops. That's what we get when we build human empires instead of God's Kingdom. But change is coming by the grace of God. May God open our spiritual eyes.

The third common factor usually responsible for the collapse of empires is the re-introduction of the gospel. This is very interesting in the sense that even those we refer to as secular writers, philosophers and activists have all agreed that the influence of the man Jesus in nation building and civilization cannot be made a trivial. By this, they are mostly referring to His life-changing universal principles which are glorious in themselves. But the main thrust of this book is Jesus' all-encompassing life and not just His principles.

Historically, it is believed that the arrival of Christianity usually minimizes and renders redundant the power of the emperors. Little wonder then that when Jesus came to the scene, the Pharisees (legalists) lost their control and business enterprise. When Paul cast out the demons from the young girl that was being used for merchandise, all hell broke loose because somebody's business was gone. (Acts 16)

I know God's words say that part of the signs of the last days are the multiplication of all these evil things, but we still have a responsibility in preventing their encroachment into our own immediate constituency to protect the flock under our covering just like the Apostles of old did. (Acts 20:28, 1 Peter 5:2)

When we become spiritually complacent and we go into spiritual apathy and lukewarmness by not preaching the Jesus-centered message of God's grace, we unintentionally open the doors for wolves in sheep's clothing to invade the church to destroy the innocent sheep. We are not talking here about brethren with certain moral weaknesses. (Although, moral weaknesses can be fixed when we constantly give Jesus to the people.) The issue here is allowing people who were not even saved in the first place infiltrate our leadership structure because the growth of our empires is more important to us than the gospel of Jesus Christ. The reason is simple. We may not want to openly admit it but the point is, the bigger our empires, the bigger our influence which is not inherently bad in itself as long as Christ is preached in all our endeavors. Unfortunately, it is like we are even more popular than the Head of the church Himself.

Again, our empires are tumbling down by force unless we repent regarding our message. This gospel revolution is about to invade the planet on a grand scale. The first Babylon came crashing when their legalistic world view colluded with the Trinitarian life. Genesis 11:7 says, *"...Let us go down and confuse their language..."*

Anything that is not in alignment with God's original vision is always going to crumble and not the other way around. Just like all the disruptive innovations going on in the world, the church world is about to witness a disruptive re-awakening of the Spirit. The oppressed masses will cry out to God, like the children of Israel in Egypt. (Exodus 2:23) The slaves will revolt in their enclaves. They may sound rebellious, ungrateful, rude and arrogant on the surface, but mature leaders with the heart of the father will look beyond their head to see the longing and the groaning of their souls.

Because of the pain, gloom, suffering, hurt and loneliness in their souls they may lack the right words to express their frustrations on social media. Majority of them don't hate Jesus, but hate religion that is killing them. Unfortunately, they may be throwing rocks at innocent leaders who themselves need to have fresh encounters with Jesus Christ.

These modern-day empires will fall just like the ones in the past. Only Jesus and His finished work of grace will remain. This gospel revolution will bring down every legalistic organization after reducing the stubborn emperors' influence. The voice of grace will be amplified in the body of Christ while every other voice that is not preaching Christ will be reduced before they go into complete silence. It is indeed an apostolic and a prophetic re-awakening. The kind that has never happened in this fashion since the world began. *"For the earnest expectation of the creation eagerly waits for the revealing of the sons of God"*. (Romans 8:19)

# *Chapter Twelve*

> *There shall be a compression of times and seasons for your sake and you will enjoy the rhythm of sowing and reaping at the same time. Instead of working and resting, there will be a supernatural reversal. You will rest and then work.*

## On the Threshold of a Revolutionary Awakening:
# TAIL PIECE

## CHAPTER
# TWELVE

## On the Threshold of a
## Revolutionary Awakening:
# TAIL PIECE

It was a bright summer afternoon in Silver Spring, Maryland. I had gone to pick our children from school. Usually, I try to arrive at least twenty minutes earlier so I can stay in the car to relax a little before the school closes. On this memorable day that I will not forget, I had an encounter with God's love that has left an indelible mark on me ever since. As these innocent 4 – 7 graders came out of the door, something that an average person including me takes for granted everyday happened. All the parents, without exception gave warm hugs and smiling faces to their children as if they had not seen them in a long time.

I was watching this beautiful, Godly scenario from my car as I waited for our children to come out. These parents from different races and backgrounds had one thing in common – they all love and cherish their children. Nothing else matters to them. Money, fame, houses, cars and all the good things of life were not as important to these parents at this time but their children. "Where do you think this love is coming from?", the Holy Spirit asked me in a gentle but firm voice. At first, I couldn't give an answer because in my spirit I knew my answer will be religiously foolish. Up till that moment, my answer would have been, "these parents can only display this kind of love to their children because they are probably Christians and because it is a private Christian school environment." But I knew I had seen similar scenarios before even in non-religious places like bars, parties and even club houses. It was the beginning of a major theological shift for me. I think this could be a revolutionary re-awakening in the church and the nations before the Lord returns.

Our heavenly Father began to show me from the word, that human beings that He created in His image and likeness are the sole expressions of the mutual love that has always existed in the Trinitarian shared life. God allowed me to have a little glimpse into the space and the world of the Father, the Son and the Spirit. This Kind of love between these parents and their children is beyond them. They do not possess the human capacity to love that way. It is a divine expression that may not be fully comprehended on this side of eternity.

This kind of love did not belong to us originally. We are not the creator or the originator. It is as ancient as the Trinity. We enjoy sharing this love with our children because we are part of God's eternal plan. If we go deeper, we even unconsciously share this love to "strangers" like our spouses, friends, neighbors, colleagues, etc. That's why we marry, have friends, trust people and want to help one another. I have seen non-religious people crying and shedding tears at the scene of accidents where people they never met died. I have also seen people rejoice with strangers at their moments of triumph. These are all expressions of different emotions that have their origins in God.

But religion has separated us from these divine realities. We exclude people with these God-created attributes from our cultic organizations because we think they don't belong to *perichoresis* simply because they don't talk like us, dress like us and agree with us. We have become the access controllers to the Trinitarian circle and we only open the gate to only those we think are qualified based on our perceived standards. But God seems to be saying "enough". When Jesus died, He didn't die for the church or any organization but for the whole world. *"For God so loved the world that He gave His only begotten Son, that whoever believes in Him should not perish but have everlasting life."* (John 3: 16)

In fact, it is so bad that we arrogantly condemn certain people to hell and exclude them from heaven on the premise of their current behaviors. I can imagine what Jesus will be saying if the early church had condemned Saul of Tarsus to hell before his encounter with Jesus. I strongly believe some of the hullabaloos going on in the body of Christ today are not new to God. Whether it is cyber warfare or social media attack on the church, our heavenly Father is aware of them all. It is part of the shaking. The body of

Christ must be purged and shaken inside out for the emergence of a glorious church. It will be a shaking of love. Everything that is not foundational will be shaken and rooted out. Our own gospel, denominational dogmas, greed, pride, worldliness and demonic love of money will be cut down. The spirit of mammon that has been enthroned both on the pulpit and in the pew will be shaken and expelled before a glorious manifestation of the true church of Jesus. Only a true, Jesus-centered church will remain.

Prophet Haggai saw this day several thousands of years ago and he penned down this prophetic declaration in Haggai 2: 6-9, *"For thus says the LORD of hosts: 'Once more (it is a little while) I will shake heaven and earth, the sea and dry land; and I will shake all nations, and they shall come to the Desire of All Nations, and I will fill this temple with glory,' says the LORD of hosts. 'The silver is Mine, and the gold is Mine,' says the LORD of hosts. 'The glory of this latter temple shall be greater than the former,' says the LORD of hosts. 'And in this place I will give peace,' says the LORD of hosts."*

Even though, most prophetic words have different variations in their interpretations, but their main contextual focus on Jesus should never be underrated. God said, "in a little while", He will shake the nations and the desire of all nations shall come...". You see, most of the people that we have excluded and are still excluding because of our false misinterpretation of God don't actually hate God. They are tired of sin. They are in pain and terror. In fact, most of the acts of sins they indulge in are their human attempts to numb the pain and the fear in their souls. We compound their problems and aggravate their pains when we tell them they don't belong because of their behaviors.

Imagine me walking to those parents mentioned in my story at the beginning of this chapter and asking them this question, "the love you demonstrate to your children now, where do you think it is coming from?" I bet many of them will admit they cannot explain it because it is so deep. May be a few of them will assume they love their children because it is

> You see, most of the people that we have excluded and are still excluding because of our false misinterpretation of God don't actually hate God. They are tired of sin. They are in pain and terror. In fact, most of the acts of sins they indulge in are their human attempts to numb the pain and the fear in their souls.

normal. The point is, it is a very creative way to engage anybody who feels he does not belong because he or she has been excluded. What a simple way to start a conversation with someone about starting relationship with Jesus.

Recently, I was interrupted by Phil, the Plumber, who came to fix the damaged faucet in our house. This kind-hearted Peruvian guy started a conversation with me after watching me for a few minutes. "You are so engrossed with your writing," he said. I looked up and saw a beautiful smile on his face as I responded, "Yes". Phil had been trying to get my attention, so he could explain what was wrong with the faucet. "Are you an author?", he asked. "Yes, by God's grace," was my short answer, thinking I could get him off my back so I could go back to my writing. But he would not let me go. He wanted to share his passion. "My overriding passion in life is to own a fishery in Peru where I will supply several restaurant chains and stores around the world", he said. Before I could respond, he brought out his I-phone and showed me several pictures of his fishing business under construction. His face lit up with excitement as he tried to live in his future. At this point, I sensed that my heavenly Father wanted to show me a practical example of what I was writing about. "Where do you think this desire for fishing comes from?", I asked him. "From my eight-year-old son who knows the name, specie and biology of every fish. He has been studying fishes from age five. I wanted to build this for him", he concluded. I explained to him that the Trinitarian shared life of the Father, the Son and the Spirit is being shared with his son who will be their expression of love to mankind. And that his son is sharing it with him. I concluded by taking him through a journey into eternity where everything began. "Imagine thousands of families having delicious dinner with Salmon or Tilapia fish from your business with excitement because they really enjoy your fish. Think about the joy the Trinity will experience when preachers like me eat your fish and are able to preach because we are eating healthy fish from a non- preacher who could supply delicious fishes. That has always been the Trinitarian vision and it has not changed". I concluded that the fisherman's desire to fish and feed people is as good as the preacher who wants to travel the world to preach the gospel of Jesus Christ. Both are expressing something beyond them. This young man looked at me with a broad smile and said, "You are a good man." But the truth is that, it is not about me. It's all about Jesus and His finished work of grace.

It is imperative for us to know that the world is not just waiting for the manifestation of preachers alone. God's word says in Romans 8:19, *"For the earnest expectation of the creation eagerly waits for the revealing of the sons of God."* The whole creation is waiting for the emergence of sons of God. Politicians alone can't solve the world's problem. Governments, independent of God's grace can't successfully legislate against sin. Sin is spiritual. Celebrities and social influencers can't resolve the global crisis in their human wisdom. In fact, we don't need more churches for the sake of churches, but we need more churches that are on the vanguard of proclaiming Jesus and His finished work of grace alone. By the time the purging, shaking and the pulling down of everything that is unholy is done, Prophet Haggai says there will be a supernatural manifestation of God's glory, wealth and peace in the church. The kind that the world has never seen. This glory will be unleashed on the earth after the shaking and the pruning which will bring Jesus back to the center stage. At this point, nothing else will matter anymore but Jesus alone.

The church of Jesus will no longer be a laughing stock. People from all nations shall flow into the glorious church without wrinkle or blemish. A church that has been perfected by the owner of the church Himself (Jesus Christ). The Jesus-focused church of the last days will be so supernaturally attractive that the people will count themselves privileged and specially favored to be part of her.

*"The word that Isaiah the son of Amos saw concerning Judah and Jerusalem. Now it shall come to pass in the latter days That the mountain of the LORD's house Shall be established on the top of the mountains, And shall be exalted above the hills; And all nations shall flow to it. Many people shall come and say, 'Come, and let us go up to the mountain of the LORD, To the house of the God of Jacob; He will teach us His ways, And we shall walk in His paths.' For out of Zion shall go forth the law, And the word of the LORD from Jerusalem."* (Isaiah 2:1-3)

According to this prophetic word from Isaiah the prophet, the grace-filled church will be established. The church of Jesus will be exalted above all other things. It will be a church in her own class all by herself in Christ. And all nations shall come to the church. This will not be about a particular denomination or about a particular superstar. We will still have fully functional ministry gifts operating in synergy with the spirit of grace in equipping the saints for the work of the ministry (Ephesians 4:8). The true apostolic church in the order of the first century church will come to the forefront again. These true apostles, prophets, evangelists, pastors and teachers will through the help of the Holy Spirit dismantle every stronghold of lie and deception that has held people in bondage for decades. There will be mass miracles, healings and more breakthroughs in science and technology orchestrated by divine ingenuity because we have the mind of Christ.

(1Corinthians 2:16). There will be divine alignments and Godly order devoid of manipulations and spiritual witchcraft.

There shall be willing submission to Godly authorities without being forced and without people losing their uniqueness. This supernatural Godly reference will be after the order of what happened between Jesus and His disciples who had different temperaments. Yet they all came to a place of spiritual maturity and were ready to sacrifice anything for the sake of the gospel. The last day church of Jesus will emerge in true holiness, greater influence and wealth without greed. The Jesus-focused church in these last days will spread faster than the speed of light. For those who are focused on Jesus alone, it may look like things are slow now, but keep looking unto Jesus, the Author and the Finisher of your faith. There shall be a compression of times and seasons for your sake and you will enjoy the rhythm of sowing and reaping at the same time. Instead of working and resting, there will be a supernatural reversal. You will rest and then work. So much so that you will not be able to take the credit for the manifestation of this glory because it will be obvious that whatever good things you are experiencing will be attributed to Jesus in you, the Hope of glory (Colossian 1 :27). Go now and live the rest of your life and express His love in whatever He has called you to do. The whole world is waiting for you. Yes, go in Christ's consciousness and His finished work of grace. Go. His grace alone is sufficient for you. Jesus is in you. You are in Him. He is for you. And He is also with you. Jesus is more than enough.

# REFERENCE

Ellis, Paul. The Gospel in Ten Words King Press, 2012

Gunn, Tricia "Unveiling Jesus LCC"

Prince, Joseph "GRACE Revolution Faith Words, 2015

Smith, Judah. "JESUS" Thomas Nelson, 2013

Trinitarian Coversation Grace Commission International, 2016

Wommack, Andrew. Grace Harrison House, 2017

Whitten, Clerk. Pure Grace, Destiny Image, 2012

# SAM ORE

Kingdom Ambassadors Church Centre
13011 Firestone Court
Silver Spring MD, 20904
**Phone:** 301-5811 or 1800-978-0520
**Email:** pastor@kacconline.org
**Website:** www.samoreministries.org, kacconline.org

Please include your testimonies or help received from reading this book.

Your prayer requests are also welcome.

You can order additional copies of this book or any other by the author online at

www.amazon.com

www.samoreministries.com

or simply send email to pastor @kacconline.org with your request.